THE UNIVERSITY OF CHICAGO
PUBLICATIONS IN ANTHROPOLOGY

*

SOCIAL ANTHROPOLOGICAL SERIES

A Village
That Chose Progress

A Village
That Chose Progress

CHAN KOM REVISITED

By

Robert Redfield

THE UNIVERSITY OF CHICAGO PRESS

THE UNIVERSITY OF CHICAGO PRESS, CHICAGO 37
Cambridge University Press, London, N.W. 1, England
W. J. Gage & Co., Limited, Toronto 2B, Canada

Copyright 1950 by The University of Chicago. All rights reserved
Published 1950. Second Impression 1957. Composed and printed
by THE UNIVERSITY OF CHICAGO PRESS, *Chicago, Illinois,*
U.S.A.

For
M. P. R.
&
J. M. R.

Preface

A T TIMES during the years from 1930 to 1933 four persons, of whom I was one, made studies of certain communities in Yucatan, Mexico, under provision made by Carnegie Institution of Washington. We were interested in the transformations taking place in the folk culture of the peninsula as civilization developed in or impinged upon the towns and villages. We studied four communities, ranging from a settlement of tribally organized Indians in east central Quintana Roo to Merida, the capital of the state of Yucatan. The more general results of these studies, and the comparisons of each with the others, were expressed in a book I wrote: *The Folk Culture of Yucatan* (Chicago: University of Chicago Press, 1941), translated as *Yucatán, una cultura en transición* (Mexico City: Fondo de Cultura Económica, 1944). Other publications, by one or another of the group of investigators, reported on particular communities studied or on special aspects of Yucatecan life.

The third of the four communities, as they are regarded as a series from the city to the tribal hinterland, is Chan Kom, a village of Indians living in well-established economic and political relationship with the state government of Yucatan and the national government of Mexico and yet, in its situation in the bush apart from roads and railroads, physically isolated from town and city. Alfonso Villa Rojas, native of Yucatan, for several years the schoolteacher of this village and now well-known anthropologist of Mexico City, came to understand and to have affection for this village and its people. He joined with me in studying the village and in making a book that describes its life as we saw it, especially in the year

1931. The book is *Chan Kom: A Maya Village*, by Robert Redfield and Alfonso Villa Rojas ("Carnegie Institution of Washington Publication," No. 448 [Washington, D.C., 1934]).

Villa and I often talked of coming back to Chan Kom after the passage of years to see what had happened to the community. The villagers had committed themselves to progress and civilization so vigorously that one wanted to know what would come of it. Dr. A. V. Kidder, head of the Division of Historical Research of Carnegie Institution, more than once spoke encouragingly of the idea of studying the village again. In the winter of 1948 I took an opportunity to do so. I spent six weeks in the village. My wife and my young son were with me. The following pages tell what we saw and learned about the changes that took place in Chan Kom in the seventeen years from 1931 to 1948. The book is a part of the biography of a community, of a people who conceived a common purpose, and of what they did to realize it. It says something interesting to me, and I think to others, of the effort we all make, in one way or another, to achieve the good life.

Of the people of Chan Kom, one especially, Sr. D. Eustaquio Ceme, appears often in the pages that follow. More than any other man he made his village what it is today. Energetic and also deeply reflective, tenacious of purpose and yet flexible, generous and kindly, he is an admirable man and a notable leader. In this book I have not attempted to conceal his identity, as I have that of other villagers; he may well take pride in what he has done. And indeed he has told his own story, of his earlier years, in a little autobiography which he wrote for me and which the reader will find published in the earlier book about Chan Kom. How much I owe to him for understanding of Chan Kom the reader of this present book will see at once when he reads it.

The Social Science Research Committee of the University of Chicago provided, out of money that came from the Rockefeller Foundation, the funds I used in making the trip last winter to Yucatan. I am by this fact indebted to the Committee, and to the University that left it to me to decide that my time last winter be spent in making this study. My friends John U. Nef, A. V. Kidder, and Alfonso Villa Rojas, among those who read the manuscript, kindly took the pains to offer suggestions as to revision; I am grateful to them and wish I could have made even fuller use of their excellent suggestions. Dr. Morris Steggerda allowed me to include some facts about Chan Kom that he noted in 1935 on one of his trips to the village. Dr. Sol Tax, friend and colleague, has been greatly helpful in seeing the book through to publication. Dr. Sylvanus G. Morley helped me with arrangements for the recent trip and, out of his devotion to the Maya and their works, cheered me on; news of his death came to me as I was about to send him the manuscript to read.

My wife, Margaret Park Redfield, who has published on aspects of the Yucatan studies made in the earlier years, worked with me in collecting the materials that are the basis of this book, in thinking about them, and in revising the manuscript. The content of the last chapter in particular owes much to her.

As chairman of the Committee on Social Thought of the University of Chicago, Mr. John U. Nef kindly allows me to say, as I am pleased and honored to do, that the Committee (with which I am associated) regards this small work as a contribution toward its objective of bringing knowledge together so that there may be developed a more unified outlook on all works of the mind.

ROBERT REDFIELD

UNIVERSITY OF CHICAGO
October 1949

Contents

VIII

CHAN KOM, ITS ETHOS AND ITS SUCCESS
Page 155

GLOSSARY
Page 179

INDEX
Page 181

I

Chan Kom Defines Its Goals

IN THE year 1917, or at about that time, the leaders of a frontier settlement of Maya Indians in southeastern Yucatan came to a decision which was critical for them and which set in motion events recorded in these pages. It was decided to convert the settlement into a pueblo. One who heard the discussion remembers that it was agreed to work to attain this end even if it should cost each man the value of a horse.

To "become a pueblo" meant to adopt many of the ways and political forms and ambitions of townspeople. It meant to accept the tools, leadership, and conceptions of progress which were then being offered to the villagers of Yucatan by the leaders of Mexico's social revolution. It required the inhabitants to give up some of the isolation which was theirs in the remote and sparsely inhabited lands that lay apart from the goings and comings of city men. In future they would be a part of the political and economic institutions of Yucatan, of Mexico, and—though of course they would not have put it so—of the one world that was then in the making.

At the time of the decision there were about a hundred people living in Chan Kom, and its history of recent and continuous settlement ran back not more than thirty years. It had been founded by pioneers: the men who made it had sought new opportunities in a wilderness and had ventured into the deeper forest not to incur new responsibilities but to escape from old ones that had become onerous. So remote were these first forest settle-

ments at their inception that among the founders of some
of them were included men escaped from servitude on
haciendas who there felt themselves safe from pursuit. The
anciently established village from which most of the
settlers of Chan Kom had come was Ebtun, situated just
west of the town of Valladolid, and about thirty miles
north of Chan Kom; they had left it because land in its
neighborhood had become scarce and poor and because
the country to the south, long left unexploited, promised
better harvests of corn and beans. They left, too, because
there had been a factional dispute in Ebtun, such as develop frequently in these Maya villages, and the emigrants
wished to escape from this dispute. Once established in
Chan Kom, the settlers found it a heavy and unwelcome
burden to return the long way to Ebtun to perform the
traditionally imposed labor on public works in a community to which their loyalties were no longer attached.
These early settlers wanted chiefly to be left alone to make
milpa in a territory where they could choose for their
cornfields the lands they liked. They did not yet grasp the
fact that by going forward to political independence of
Ebtun they might have the freedom they wanted, and
they were not yet ready to assume the responsibilities
which becoming a pueblo would bring upon them. So,
when it was first proposed to them that they become a
pueblo, they said "No."

The first men to come to Chan Kom, in the memory of
the people who lived there in 1917, were three of Ebtun
who came about 1880 and put their houses of wattle and
thatch around the cenote, one of those natural wells which
everywhere in early Yucatan were the only sources of
water and the inevitable centers of settlements. The connection with Ebtun continued for several decades: the
few settlers at Chan Kom were thought of, and thought of
themselves, as a mere *ranchería*—a collection of milpas

and houses under the authority of and dependent upon the parent-community of Ebtun. By the first decade of the twentieth century there were still only three or four houses; other men came and made milpa at Chan Kom but returned to their families and houses in Ebtun. But, as the first years of the twentieth century went by, more of these men built houses at Chan Kom and remained there. By the time of the critical decision, the leadership of the community had passed from the first three settlers to the heads of three more recently arrived families: the Cemes, the Pats, and the Tamays. All three families had come from Ebtun, and they were linked in kinship: the wife of Guillermo Tamay was a sister of the three Ceme brothers; the father of the three Pat brothers was the *compadre* of the father of the three Ceme brothers; and Eustaquio Ceme, an orphaned nephew of these Cemes, had just married one of the Pat girls. These leaders of the community in 1917 were young men, in their twenties or thirties; this can happen in a community of pioneers. The Pat men had not learned Spanish, but several of the Ceme men had some knowledge of the language, learned for the most part in a school in Ebtun, and Guillermo Tamay had lived for a time with a priest and from him had learned prayers of the Catholic ritual. It may be safely assumed that none of the women spoke Spanish.

The settlers came into a land which was wilderness. It had been abandoned because of the ravages and dangers of the "War of the Castes," that struggle between Indians and whites that began in 1847 and that never came to any definitive end. Some of the Indians remained unreconciled to white domination and retreated into the high forests of Quintana Roo. The rest went back to work as serfs and later as free laborers on plantations and to live in such villages as Ebtun. The land between remained uninhabited for many years. Slowly repopulation began. Groups of

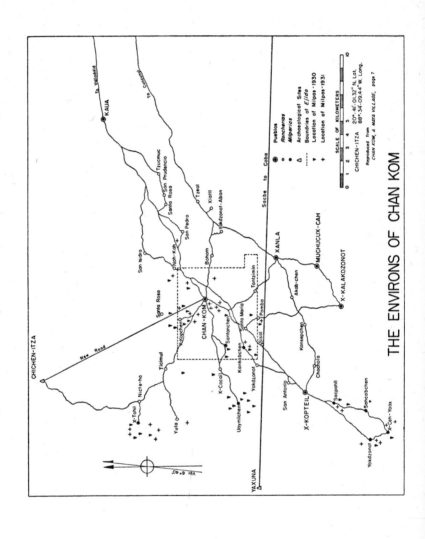

THE ENVIRONS OF CHAN KOM

CHICHEN-ITZA

To Valladolid

KAUA

To Cenotul

Tzucmuc

San Prudencio

Tzeal

Santa Rosa

Xiatil

San Pedro

Yokdzonot-Aban

San Isidro

Nóh-Káh

Bohom

Santa Rosa

Ticimul

CHAN-KOM

New Road

Tontzimin

X-Dzopchen

Sontonchen

Santa Maria

Pomba

Nicte-ha

Santa Rosa

Yula

X-Cocal

Kankabchen

Sisal

XANLA

Akab-chen

X-Tohil

Uaymilchen

Yokdzonot

San Antonio

Kansechen

Chachola

MUCHUCUX-CAH

X-KALAKDZONOT

Sacbe to Coba

San Antonio

Sacpahli

X-KOPTEIL

Sohcobchen

Yokdzonot

X-Cen-Yoox

YAXUNA

Var. 6°-40'

	Pueblos
●	Rancherias
○	Milperias
△	Archaeological Sites
---	Boundaries of Ejido
▶	Location of Milpas·1930
+	Location of Milpas·1931

SCALE OF KILOMETERS

0 1 2 3 4 5   10

CHICHEN-ITZA   20°-41'-01.32" N. Lat.
88°-34'-09.4" W. Long.

Reproduced from
CHAN KOM, A MAYA VILLAGE, page 7

three or four families came south and east, and tiny settlements were made at Tzucmuc, Santa Maria, Cosil, Ton-Tzimin, and Chan Kom. Chan Kom was settled on the northwest edge of this unoccupied territory. "When my father was five years old," said one of the older men in later years, referring to the period of about 1880, "there were only three or four houses at Chan Kom. No one lived in Ticimul, or in Ticincacab, or in X-Kopteil, or in Xanla, because Chan Kom was the last settlement here." By 1925 many other settlements had sprung up in the abandoned territory, yet no significant community had been established farther into the wilds than was Chan Kom, for an engineer who came to make surveys in that year wrote: "It is the last large settlement of the Department of Valladolid before entering the territory of Quintana Roo." In northern Quintana Roo there were no large settlements and very, very few small ones. Chan Kom lay upon the frontier.

The land was wilderness, but it was familiar. It was covered with the same thorny bush, providing the same kind of firewood and building materials, that the settlers already knew. In it stood the tall wine-palms to show them where the rich lands were; and other trees and plants were familiar, as their many different uses, in medicine or in ritual, were familiar. The cenotes were in kind familiar, and some of them, although yet to be rediscovered in the dense bush, had names that were known through their occurrence in traditional prayers recited by the shaman priests when the ceremony to bring rain was held in times of threatened drought on the outskirts of the young settlement. In the new land the settlers found pits from which to dig crumbled limestone of which to make the lime needed to soften the corn for grinding. They hunted the same kinds of deer and agouti they had known before and sought the wild bees and the trees to hollow out to serve as hives—all as they had known them before. The land was familiar, and men had lived in it before. The settlers found the vestiges of walls that had been used as ramparts in the "War of the Castes" and overgrown clearings where fruit trees had been planted. They found also the low mounds built of stones, about which occurred fragments of pottery figures and pieces of obsidian. These told of still earlier dwellers in this region in a period so remote that the settlers had been taught by their elders that the builders of these mounds had been a long-vanished race with miraculous powers, unconnected with men of these times. The obsidian flakes, the settlers knew, were the projectiles used by the invisible guardians of the clearings in the bush, the balams, in keeping off the ever present threateners of evil, the intangible winds that emanate from caves, from snakes, from watery clouds, and that attend the invisible deities of the forest and forest trails. The new land was to be worked and to be read like the old one.

The hesitation of these settlers to accept the proposal of the revolutionary leaders that Chan Kom become a pueblo probably arose from their fear of losing the independence they had won on the frontier. The new community was disposed to turn its attention to the land of old meanings and new resources. The people wanted chiefly to be let alone. If the subordination to Ebtun was burdensome, there would be burdens to bear in making Chan Kom a pueblo, a village politically recognized in the new government of the *dzules*, the white people of the towns. Why should the settlers, in their freedom, accept from a distant national government formal recognition of their rights to certain communal lands—*ejidos*—with the implication that other lands also convenient for the making of milpa were not available to Chan Kom and with the prospects of extending regulation of the affairs of the settlement by outside authority? The dozen or two families of the settlement must have doubted the wisdom of the decision they eventually made, or they would not first have refused to become a pueblo.

The suggestion was made to them when they came to ask Felipe Carrillo Puerto, governor of Yucatan, for furniture for their school. The military commander at Valladolid had taken an interest in the young settlement and in 1910 had sent a teacher to Chan Kom. I do not know through what difficulties or successes the school passed in the next ten years. They were the ten years in which Mexico overthrew the old government of Díaz and his local military commanders and inaugurated great political, economic, and social reforms. In 1918 Alvarado, leader of the Revolution in Yucatan, had been succeeded by Carrillo Puerto, who, even more than his predecessor, reached out into the rural communities to draw the Maya *milperos* into the new society. In that year, probably, some of the men of Chan Kom came to the governor to ask him to provide furniture for their little school. He told them that there was furniture only in the pueblos and that, if his visitors would turn their settlement into a pueblo, he would see that they got furniture. They told Carrillo Puerto that they did not want to do this.

And yet it was not long thereafter—certainly less than a year—before the village leaders had changed their minds and had begun to work, with a determination and an enthusiasm that have distinguished the village ever since, to make the settlement not only a pueblo but the most important and powerful community in this part of the frontier region.

What has been told me of the making of the decision is not enough to show just how and why the ultimate decision was made. It must have been difficult not to make it, for the "incorporation of the Indian" into the revolutionary Mexican society was firm policy and was nowhere more vigorously asserted than in Yucatan, where the peons on many of the henequen haciendas had been treated with unusual harshness and where the revolutionary leaders strove to liberate not only the Indian's body but also his mind and his courage. For a year or more the Chan Kom people had heard the propaganda of the Revolution, had heard that the land belonged to the Indian and was to be returned to him, and that progress, in the form of tools, schools, music, and prosperity was desirable and would be extended to any village that became a pueblo and followed the leadership of the Socialist party. The Chan Kom people wanted freedom, and the Revolutionary government of Yucatan offered, it said, freedom, and proved its good will by gifts of tools, drums, flags, and furniture—to those settlements that became pueblos.

And still unresolved was that struggle with Ebtun. More and more the Chan Kom settlers resented the authority over them of a distant village and the obligation to labor in the parent-community on public works which, as residents in Chan Kom, they would not themselves enjoy. The resentment of the people of Ebtun against the disobedient and thriving daughter-settlement was correspondingly strong. If Chan Kom should be recognized by the new government of Yucatan as a pueblo, it would have its own governmental officer, its *comisario*, and could then compel public service in Chan Kom itself under its own officers. Then its men would no longer have to carry their dried tortillas nine leagues through the bush to Ebtun to labor on public works in that now half-hostile community. To "become a pueblo" would be to engage themselves in the obligations of formal government, but, to a degree, it would be self-government. To accept the proposals of the state authorities would be to assume new obligations, but it would make them free of Ebtun.

Pioneers though they were, their tradition was not one of initiative and independence by separate individuals. These Maya had always lived under rule, authority, discipline. In earlier centuries the mission, and early and late the hacienda, had managed and compelled their mode of life. They might resent the occasional cruelties of this rule, but they were used to formal and legal order and discipline and had taken it into their private lives. They punished their erring sons with the lash and on occasions, as a public responsibility, erring husbands and wives too. They had long been used to bring their more serious difficulties to authorities outside their local and personal existence: to masters or to governmental officers. The tradition of these people combined the authority of spontaneous and unformulated custom with formal and legal regulation imposed from above.

These people were not rebels; they still wanted to be part of the world in which lay their parent-villages. They had by no means severed the ties that bound them to the villages of the north. They had kinsmen in those villages, and, remote as they were in their new settlements, they returned to the fiestas of Ebtun and Uayma, and they drove their cattle to Valladolid to sell there.

So they decided to become a pueblo. They agreed to admit engineers to their settlement to survey the land that would be registered in the city as their communal property. They followed the instructions of the state government in organizing a Socialist League, a unit within the new political structure that the Socialist party was building in Yucatan. They were prepared to send representatives to meetings of the party in Merida and to pay the small dues of membership. It was explained to them that they were to vote in state and national elections, and they soon came to understand that this was another of the many formalities, the many sendings and receivings of documents, which admittance into the new civilization entailed. They received drums, a trumpet, and dynamite to blast the rocks from the stony hillocks where they would make the plaza of the pueblo they had yet to build.

Chan Kom began a course of deliberate self-improvement in which, above all other similar settlements of the region, it was to excel. Indeed, the pre-eminence of the village, according to the accounts, was already indicated even before the inhabitants began to make a pueblo. Theirs was the first of the frontier communities to have a school, and some settlers in neighboring *rancherías* were attracted to Chan Kom because of its school. The settlement was early known as one of sober and honest men, and the traders from Valladolid who were now beginning to come down into the southeast to sell manufactured goods and to buy hogs and fowl made Chan Kom a place in which to spend the night. A year after the village leaders had filed their formal petition for the communal lands (in 1923), the Chan Kom people were drawn into bloody conflict between the Socialists, on the one hand, and the *Liberales*, the conservative opponents of the new regime, on the other. Locally this was also a conflict between the people of the Chan Kom region and those of Yaxcaba and Sotuta, to the west. These two regions had anciently belonged to different native Indian chieftainships; although the Chan Kom people had only shadowy memory of the fact that they belonged to the realm of the Cupuls while their enemies had anciently belonged in the territory of the Cocoms, I think that some tradition of enmity contributed to the drawing of the alignments in 1924. When the people of X-Kopteil, a settlement within the Chan Kom area of friendship and sympathy, were attacked, and then when a man of Chan Kom was struck down in his own cornfield, the Pats and the Tamays and the Cemes went off to war.

The participation of Chan Kom in the war was brief but not inglorious. One result of the conflict was to bring to Chan Kom several families of Yaxcaba who were on the side of the *socialistas*. Thus was expressed, in violent form, that endless struggle among the Maya settlements: a factional dispute within a settlement is resolved by the victory of one party; those of the defeated party take refuge and establish residence in some neighboring village that has given aid to their party for reasons arising from the rivalry between the two settlements. This pattern of conflict, withdrawal, and resettlement is repeated again and again; it is a mechanism whereby the bold and vigorous settlement, the settlement that defends itself and takes up the interests of its friends in other settlements, grows strong at the expense of its rivals. Within the span of years covered in this little chronicle, only in the time of the Revolution did this pattern express itself in armed violence. In the later years it was no less manifest, but in the form of competition to attain the status of pueblo or independent municipality, or of struggle between parties within a hamlet to attach the settlement to this pueblo or to that. Here politics has been the continuation of war.

The little war did not long delay the formalities attending the conversion of Chan Kom into a pueblo. In 1925 its lands were surveyed, and in 1926 the inhabitants were put in formal possession of their lands. The event was a ceremony signalizing new status rather than the acquisition of new agricultural resources. For forty years the inhabitants, however few, had made their cornfields in these lands and in other lands outside the tract now made legally theirs; but the grant of the *ejido* had been established by revolutionary leaders as the event signalizing the admission of the village community into the free and progressive socialist state. The grant of an *ejido* was the

occasion of a celebration in the honored village: the celebration was attended characteristically by representatives
of the state or the national government; flags, music, and
speeches marked the coming-of-age of the community.
Chan Kom, as the first settlement in its territory to attain
the status, gained fresh prestige, and additional families
came to make their residence there. It should be mentioned that to take residence in a Yucatecan pueblo is not
simply to make one's house and home there. It is to become enrolled in a community of men enjoying common
rights and subject to common obligations—rights to a
house lot and to make milpa in the common lands and
obligations to obey the local authorities and especially to
perform the labor required, regularly and also on special
occasions, for the common good.

In the meantime the villagers had been working to make
their settlement take on the material characteristics of a
Spanish town. They cut down trees from the land around
the cenote and used the dynamite given them to blast
away the rocky hills. Here they would make a plaza.
Streets were sketched out in the uneven and stony bush;
some of the inhabitants moved their thatched huts down
to face upon these streets; the one man in the village who
knew something about the mason's art began to build the
first houses of stone and mortar upon the clearing that
would be the plaza. In 1927 one of the men of the community with more corn to sell than others put some of the
money from the sale of his corn into the digging of the
first well.

Meanwhile the school had continued to function, although somewhat erratically. We could learn nothing as to
the influence of the teachers who came to Chan Kom before 1927; there were eight of them in seven years, and
not much good was said of them to us. In 1917 a school
building had been constructed: a long, dirt-floored struc-

ture with low stone walls and high, low-hanging thatched roof. In 1927 there arrived a teacher who was to stay for four years. He was a young man in need of a job who had left college before taking his degree to serve for little pay as teacher in this remote settlement. He had not lived among villagers, and he did not speak Maya. Whatever had been said to him about how to find the village in which he was to teach had not been very clearly said, and he wasted twenty-four hours in following misleading directions. When he rode into the village one afternoon, the doors were shut against him by mothers who had formed their impressions of teachers from his predecessors; alone he sought out and recognized the building that served as a school, and there he hung up his hammock. This is the story not of Alfonso Villa Rojas but of the village of Chan Kom. By 1930 the villagers had found in the new teacher a man whom they could trust and admire. When there came to the village government letters or documents that puzzled the leaders, the teacher helped them to understand and helped them to do what they decided to do, without doing any of the deciding himself. When the Ebtun people, angry anew with Chan Kom over a source of conflict perennial in the region—the trespass of the cattle of one village on the milpas of another—threatened to attack Chan Kom with force of arms, the teacher spent a night with the other defenders of the village behind low walls erected in earlier wars. In the house where he came to be lodged and fed, the teacher talked about the care and feeding of children or about Yucatecan politics and read the newspaper and spoke of what it contained. And in 1930 he was talking in Maya.

During these years something was going on which drew the attention of the Chan Kom people in a new direction. A strange people were working in the ruins of ancient buildings at Chichen Itza. Chichen Itza, then distant from

Chan Kom by about twenty kilometers of bush trail, was well known to the people of Chan Kom for the great structures of stone, built long ago by a vanished race, who worked at night, when the stone was soft, and made the stones come into place by whistling to them whistles the the knowledge of which has been lost in this age of travail. It was said that these people—the Itzas, were they? or the Chac Uincob, the Red People?—would come back some day; and there had been those who said, when Felipe Carrillo Puerto spoke to the villagers about the progress that was to be theirs, when they had made pueblos, that he, perhaps, was the king of the Itzas, returned. Now there were *americanos* doing things among these ruins. These *americanos*, a tall, red, loud people, had unusual powers too. They drove trucks and motorcycles; they brought down strange food and machinery to the old hacienda where Don Eduardo had lived; and they made the stones of the old buildings come back into their places. Chichen lay in a direction opposite to that in which the Chan Kom people ordinarily went when they left Chan Kom for town or city. Their usual route was east, to Cuncunul and Valladolid, towns holding the authorities to which Chan Kom was responsible, and toward the villages of their first homeland. Westward lay less trodden trails and the towns and villages of an alien territory. One man, who had come to Chan Kom from Yaxcaba when the fighting occurred in 1924, began to sell eggs to these new people at Chichen, and two or three other Chan Kom men followed his example. In the kitchens at the hacienda where the Americans lived they saw immense stores of canned foods and preserved meats, a machine to keep foods from spoiling, and other evidences of skill and power. These sellers of eggs brought to Chan Kom the news, also, that these Americans had at Chichen a little hospital where a woman treated sick or wounded people and charged nothing for it.

The people of Chan Kom began to pay more attention to Chichen Itza.

They asked their teacher about these Americans. At first Villa did not encourage them in extending their contacts with the foreigners. They were foreign to him too. He told them that federal schoolteachers were not to have anything to do with Americans; they had fought an unjust war with Mexico. A gift of food sent to Chan Kom by the nurse (Miss Kathryn MacKay) was misunderstood, and the food thrown away.

The nurse rode about the country, exploring the settlements, offering medicine and help, joining in the dances at festivals, and making friends. She rode to Chan Kom; her friendliness prevailed over suspicion; some of the Chan Kom women talked to her, and she was liked. She showed her friendliness to the teacher, and he came to visit the archeologists at Chichen Itza. There Sylvanus G. Morley opened his generous nature to the young man, sharing with him his enthusiasm for the ancient Maya, and showing his interest in their descendants among whom Villa had come to live. When Villa rode back to Chan Kom, he brought with him books Morley had lent him about the ancient civilization, and these he read in the evening, lying in his hammock.

It was these last events that brought about the choice of Chan Kom as one of four communities in which to study the ways of life in Yucatan: the task given me by Carnegie Institution of Washington. The village was chosen to represent village life in southeastern Yucatan: a life dependent upon the markets and the authorities of the city and yet shaped by a local, long-established, unwritten tradition. The relative progressiveness of Chan Kom was not a reason for its selection. The associations established with the Americans at Chichen and the presence of a teacher who was soon to become an ethnological collaborator determined the choice.

During my stay in the village from January to May, 1931, the Americans had come to be well regarded in Chan Kom. The wave of enthusiasm for progress was reaching its crest; the Americans were progressive; they had skills and knowledge which Chan Kom could use. So each American visitor from Chichen—ethnologist, sociologist, physical anthropologist, student of the Maya language, investigator of tropical diseases—was welcomed with cordiality and respectful formality, and some were invited to make improving speeches on technical or scientific subjects. These visits of the Americans took place chiefly in the years 1930–33. (Dr. Morris Steggerda spent another period in the village in 1935.) It was suggested in conversations among the villagers that perhaps these Americans were the "Red People," achieving extraordinary things today as they did in the ancient times told about by the old people. Some of the men of Chan Kom came to Chichen to ask the archeologists to help them in their efforts to improve their village. The power and accomplishments of these foreigners came to be incorporated into the villagers' dream of progress. Dissatisfied with the crooked and roundabout trail that connected their village with Chichen, and with their interests now directed to the city and toward the sources of progressive guidance by way of Chichen Itza rather than by way of Valladolid, the Chan Kom men cleared a road straight through the bush, using as their object of guidance the top of the *Castillo*, the principal ancient structure at Chichen, which they could just see from a tower they erected near their village. The road was laid, "straight as the roads of the leaf-cutter ants"; and the people called it "the road to the light." It proved impossible to use this road in its entirety, for it ran over very rough terrain; but soon another trail, using in part the straight road and more direct than the old one, was cut to Chichen and became the road chiefly used by Chan Kom people from that time on. The Chan Kom people persevered in their efforts to make a pueblo, a progressive pueblo. "We will make a village just like the Americans," a Chan Kom leader said at about this time to his people, "and if more land is needed, the government will give it."

These were the chief events which occurred in the village between the time of the decision made to convert the isolated bush settlement into a pueblo, a civilized community, and the year 1931, in which were made most of the observations that went into the book written by Villa and me about Chan Kom. The book describes a community already outstanding among its neighbors in the realized determination to progress. The book reports some of the changes accordingly made in the community. But chiefly the book is about the customs, institutions, and beliefs which the settlers brought with them from Ebtun and other villages like it. Into the community, first of pioneers in a wilderness and then of pioneers in adopting many of the ways of city people, was brought by its settlers a culture, well integrated, and represented in the mode of living of all its inhabitants.

The events of the next seventeen years carried the community still farther forward on the "road to the light." As many of them will be referred to again in the following pages, they need be only briefly recorded here. In 1931 the first commercially minded outsider—a trader from Valladolid—was permitted to settle in the village and open a store. Baseball first appeared in the village about 1929; a basketball was sent to the village by the state government in 1931. In that same year a new school building was begun, a two-room structure of masonry. When it collapsed in course of construction, killing one man and injuring several, the enthusiasm of the people for public improvements was chilled. But then an event of far-reaching importance took place: A Protestant Evangelical missionary appeared in Chan Kom, and first several families and then most of the inhabitants adopted the new religion. The determination of the people was renewed, and, in spite of the calamity that had befallen the first school building and the failure of the outside government to provide help in the work, the construction of the building was begun again, and on this second effort the people completed the work.

During 1932 and 1933 the efforts of the community were put forward toward realization of a political objective grander than any they had yet embraced: the attainment of status as a "free municipality." A pueblo is a village incorporated into the political system of Yucatan after the Revolution; it is a community with its own officers, chosen by that community. But it is one of perhaps a score of such communities all of which are attached to and dependent on a single village, paramount in that area, where is lodged the local authority for them all. This paramount village is the *cabeçera;* it, with its dependent pueblos and *rancherías,* is a *municipio;* in the language of the Revolution the *municipio* is "free"—it has its own president, its own judge, in most cases it dispenses its own justice. A *municipio* is the political recognition of the local community, the settlements of closest association and intimacy in an area of perhaps two thousand square kilometers; it is a little state within a big state. Since its detachment from Ebtun, to which pueblo it had been a *ranchería,* Chan Kom had been a pueblo belonging to the *municipio* of Cuncunul. But the Chan Kom people had moved far out from Cuncunul, and they had none of them come from that place. They had few ties of sympathy with Cuncunul, and their spirit of independence moved them to cast off this bond too. So they now strove to bring about the detachment from the *municipio* of Cuncunul of that block of settlements that most closely surrounded Chan Kom and to bring about the establishment of a new *municipio* composed of these settlements with Chan Kom as its *cabeçera*.

The matter was pushed with the state and national authorities throughout 1932, 1933, and 1934. The opposition of Cuncunul was expected and strongly countered. The rapid advances of Chan Kom in that area were the best basis for the new claim. The fact that the outlet for travelers and goods from Chan Kom to Merida was now to the west, away from Cuncunul, rather than toward it, as had been the case before, gave support to it. For several years a road had been under construction from Merida to Chichen Itza. In 1934 this road was opened; busses began regular and then daily operation between Chichen and Merida; the time of travel for the people of Chan Kom to Merida was at once reduced, from at least twenty-four hours, by way of Valladolid, including a trip of fifty kilometers on foot, to a trip of ten hours, including twenty kilometers on foot. A new trail to Chichen reduced the walking distance to fourteen kilometers. The movement of corn and hogs and eggs from Chan Kom to Merida very greatly increased.

In 1935 the new *municipio* was created, with Chan Kom as its head. An office of Civil Registry was established, to which came people from all the settlements of the new *municipio* to register births, deaths, marriages, and divorces. A post office was opened, and mail was now carried, three times weekly, between Chan Kom and Chichen. The first municipal president was Eustaquio Ceme, the second was another Ceme, and the third was a Tamay. The second or third would have been a Pat, had not the division of the community into Protestants (including the Pats) and

Catholics (including the Cemes and the Tamays) occurred at this time. The next five years were taken up with
the problems arising from this religious schism and with
those involved in maintaining the authority and the actual
continuance of the new municipality. Dissidents in
X-Kopteil and other pueblos of the new *municipio* strove
to bring about the detachment of certain of these pueblos
and *rancherías* from Chan Kom, and their reattachment to
Cuncunul, or their attachment to Yaxcaba to the west.
The effort again brought the community to the edge of
violence, but the federal government sent soldiers to Chan
Kom, and with this support the Chan Kom leaders weathered the new storm.

In 1941 the first gristmill was placed in operation, putting a hundred handmills into disuse or occasional use and
changing the work habits of as many women. In 1943 and
1944 drought, and a plague of locusts, brought near-
famine to the countryside. Chan Kom, the community of
the area with the most corn accumulated in its granaries,
and with the enterprise and knowledge which made it possible for its men to bring down from Merida quantities of
wheat flour and to bake bread for the hungry people,
gained prestige—and wealth. In 1944 the village became
the seat, for about sixteen months, of a cultural mission:
one of those temporary centers of technical and cultural
instruction which the federal government was putting into
the backward villages of the Republic. The mission consisted of ten people, all but one Yucatecans. They taught
carpentry, breadbaking, leatherworking, and the digging
of wells; they brought along a small medicine chest and
were supposed to improve the habits and knowledge of the
community in matters of hygiene; they taught the playing
of musical instruments and organized and carried out
"cultural programs" in which the young people recited
verses, enacted little dramas, and represented in feather

headdresses their own neglected ancestors. The mission painted some murals on the walls of the school and adorned the walls of some private houses with conventional borders in bright colors. One outdoor theater—a platform of masonry—had been built in an earlier year under the leadership of a teacher; now the cultural mission built another. The purpose of the mission was to stimulate the people of Chan Kom and surrounding settlements to carry out, under their own powers after the mission should leave, a mode of life, both practical and cultural, more desirable than that they had carried on before. The mission did not take the place of the school; it supplemented the activities of the school, which now took the services of two teachers, man and wife. In 1946 the mission moved on to other fields.

Chan Kom had attained its loftiest political objective. It had become the head of its own municipality. It had made itself into a pueblo, a community of dwellers—some of them—in masonry houses. It had a municipal building, with a stone jail; a school building, also of masonry; a masonry church—and a masonry Protestant chapel. It had two gristmills and four stores. It had two outdoor theaters and a baseball diamond.

The village had been the object of educational and missionary activity almost continuously, and very variously, throughout thirty years. Its people had listened to socialist propaganda in the second and third decades of the century. It had been told that alcohol was an evil and that the registration of communal lands was an indispensable honor on the road to progress. It had heard Americans talk to them of vitamins and birth control. It had listened, or failed to listen, to a long sequence of teachers, all of whom had used Spanish readers stressing national patriotism and the cultivation of the soil. It had experienced a campaign, under national auspices, to abolish illiteracy.

The officers of its local government had received, month by month, or oftener, posters, bulletins, and periodicals explaining and preaching about diversified agriculture, forestry, soil conservation, malaria, alcoholism, and hoof-and-mouth disease. It had received and responded to evangelists who taught that the cult of the *santos* was sinful, along with dancing and burning candles in a church. And after that, for nearly a year and a half, it had received within the bosom of the community a large group of professional teachers of a more modern and culturally variegated way of life.

Throughout all these experiences its leaders had maintained, almost without lapse, a favorable attitude toward proposals of reform. Those members of the community who were unwilling to follow this leadership, for the most part left it. Experiencing a long series of teachers and reformers, the community remained, above other villages, hospitable to the new and willing to listen. For was not this progress, and would not progress make Chan Kom great?

There is no wonder in the fact that Chan Kom decided to become a pueblo. Sooner or later nearly every settlement containing a score or more of houses in this part of Yucatan became a pueblo, or tried to, under leadership provided from the city and under the stimulus of ambition and desire for material advantage. What is notable is the unusual zeal with which the Chan Kom people, above all others in the neighborhood, worked to attain their objective and the outstanding success they achieved. Once they had made the decision, they set their feet firmly on the path to progress, and no exertion was too great, no discipline too firm, for the enterprise. Beginning as a cluster of thatched huts deep in the bush, no different from several others similarly situated, in the course of thirty years the village became the recognized and authoritative com-

munity of an area fifty miles across. The story of Chan
Kom is a story of success. And, like all success stories, it
suggests two questions. One is the question: What brought
about the success? Why, among the many who started, did
this one first arrive? The other question is: What is the
meaning of this success to the people of Chan Kom? Was
this that they attained really what they were striving for?
And now that it is attained, do they find it the reward they
thought it would be? This village is a village of primitive
agriculturalists, living substantially without literature,
and carrying on their lives according to tradition. On the
other hand, it is different from those quite isolated communities of tribesmen whose ways of life are repeated with
little change as the generations succeed each other and
who have, we may assume, no explicit public policy of
social change. Chan Kom, primitive though it is in many
respects, formed a public policy to change itself and thereafter bent its efforts to bring about this change. Chan Kom
decided to progress. And one may suppose that when a
people decide what they want to become in future, and
then do, in some degree, change themselves accordingly,
then at this later time, being different from what they
were before, the goals they formed earlier may not look to
them quite as they did when they formed them. In the
case of changing people—and what few people are now not
changing?—life is lived in two dimensions: the what-is and
the what-it-is-desired-to-be. And the latter, the goals and
ideals, change as the former changes. Chan Kom, reaching
success, having become different from what it was, might
differently view its success at the later date from the way
it viewed it when, a generation before, it conceived it. This,
at least, is one question that occurred to one who came to
the village for a second visit seventeen years after the first.
    In these respects the experience of Chan Kom is not so
different from the experience of most of us, especially in the

Western world. To set a goal, to make a program of self-advancement, to define that progress in terms of more material wealth, power, comfort, and health, to strive for political and economic power in competition with one's neighbors—this is what most of us have been doing. Chan Kom has been doing it in a very little way and in a very short space of time. In this little community the consequences are more plainly seen, and the record is easier to read. To return to Chan Kom in 1948, after having known the community, directly or indirectly, since its beginnings, is like seeing a large story writ small and plain. Chan Kom seems to tell us something about civilization, about civilization and some few of its discontents, that is relevant elsewhere.

II

Instruments of Living, Old and New

DURING the course of a generation Chan Kom has changed its physical aspect from that of an Indian bush settlement to that of a Spanish town. No change that has occurred there is more conspicuous, and probably none, among physical changes, has had greater consequences. A bush village is composed of houses with walls made of poles and roofs of thatch, in the form traditional and long characteristic of Indian Yucatan. These houses, in the village that has not become a pueblo, are irregularly disposed at distances convenient to the occupants in drawing water from the cenote, the center of settlement. Each house is perhaps a hundred, or two hundred, feet from its nearest neighbor. There are no streets and no regular pattern of walled yards; generally speaking, hogs and fowl go where they will and commonly enter the houses. The settlement is without buildings of general or public use, except perhaps for a hut sheltering a common altar. The bush village has no plan; it is obedient to no ideal conception.

The Spaniards brought a design for civilized living in towns and imposed it upon the Indians. They brought the scattered population together in larger settlements, and they decreed the form these were to take. A sixteenth-century document quoted by a historian of Yucatan describes this design as it was then and as it is today:

One of the things that have impeded, and impedes, the temporal and spiritual advance of the natives of these provinces is the living

25

apart one from another in the bush. I therefore order that all the natives of this province come together in pueblos, and make their houses together, arranged in pueblo form all those of one territory and principal settlement in one convenient and comfortable place; and that they make their houses of stone, and of enduring workmanship, each inhabitant's house to himself, within the tract which may be given him; and that they do not plant any milpas within the pueblo, but this be very clean, and without groves of trees; but they should cut down all such, except some fruit trees. . . .[1]

When Chan Kom decided to become a pueblo, its inhabitants at once began to rebuild their settlement into this form. A plaza, about three hundred feet on a side, was laid out to include the cenote; the lines of the first streets were indicated, and short pieces of heavy stone wall were set at the four corners of the central square to represent the blocks of contiguous masonry houses that were to be built. By 1931 the new form was clearly indicated although not realized. The plaza had been cleared of trees but not of rocky hillocks. Nine masonry houses, all on the plaza, had been built and were occupied, and four more were under construction. About half of the remaining houses, of poles and thatch, had been moved or constructed so as to align themselves with others and to face close upon the street. The first of those public buildings which take up at least one side of the plaza in Spanish-American towns was built —the *cuartel*, or building for public civil affairs. The village altar was still housed in a thatched structure set near the cenote without regard for the pueblo plan.

In 1948, as compared with 1931, the number of streets, measured in blocks, that had been at least marked out and cleared of bush had more than doubled. The village had been composed of two complete square blocks and eight or nine beginnings of squares; now there were eight such complete squares and a corresponding fringe of incomplete streets. Westward, along the old path to the

---

1. D. L. Cogolludo, *Historia du Yucatán* (Merida, 1867–68), Book I, p. 474.

cemetery, a street lined with houses had been built with such a distinct remoteness from the plaza that its inhabitants—chiefly people who had come to Chan Kom from a single neighboring settlement—referred to their neighborhood, in the manner of the people of towns, as a *colonia;* the term was generally adopted. Every building that now stood on the plaza was of masonry; on two sides these buildings presented, almost, the continuous low plastered façade of the Spanish town. A church and a school had been added to the public structures on the east side of the plaza. Upon the plaza, now almost entirely cleared of trees, was erected an outdoor theater; later a second was added; a baseball diamond was laid out. Twenty-two of the seventy-three families now occupied masonry houses, and some stone houses were to be found in every quarter of the community. The settlement around the plaza had come to take on the rectilinearity and the flat, sun-reflecting opaqueness of the Spanish-American street. The façade of stone houses now shut from the view of the passer-by much of what lay behind; the fowl pens, the beehives, the women washing clothes on their washing boards, that are so often visible to the traveler through the bush village, now receded, as it were, from view. The houses, as they closed ranks on the plaza, made four walls to bound the public, patent, and frequented central square. At the same time rectangles of land behind the houses came to be marked with low walls; the patio was coming into being, the patio that closes the domestic life away from the street while, through the setting of house close to house, it brings that life nearer than it was to the notice of its adjacent neighbors.

The change in architecture is as much and as necessary a symbol of the advanced status of the community as it is an instrument for carrying on its enlarged functions. Tradition associates authority and political dominance with

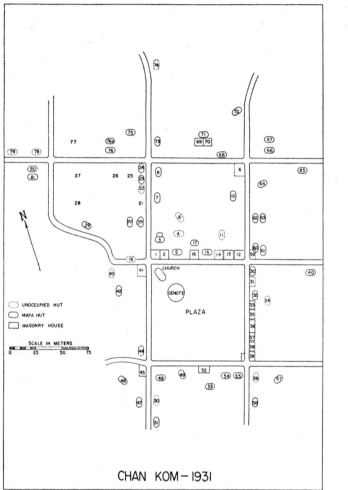
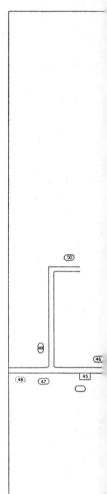

CHAN KOM — 1931

28

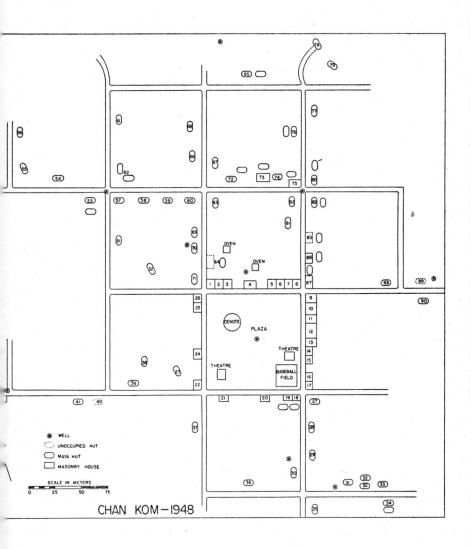

WELL
UNOCCUPIED HUT
MAYA HUT
MASONRY HOUSE

SCALE IN METERS
0   25   50   75

CHAN KOM—1948

29

this Spanish form of town. If the surrounding pueblos and *rancherías* were to accept Chan Kom as the seat of their government, Chan Kom not only must have buildings in which to hold its public meetings and its legal proceedings but must have the impressive appearance of the proper seat of such authority. If Chan Kom had not made itself look like a Spanish-American town, it could not have become a pueblo and then the headquarters of a *municipio*. It is part of the truth to say that the masonry school and the church had been added as necessary symbols of authority, as the boys who serve as police have been provided with brass badges and as a bell and a trumpet have been added to the equipment of the municipal building. No one suggests that anything be done to exclude from the plaza the great numbers of pigs, poultry, and occasional cattle and horses that roam there unrestrained, for such is the condition of the plazas in towns of greater prestige than Chan Kom, and no stigma attaches to it as yet.

If one considers the probable effects of attainment of the Spanish-American form of town upon the social organization of Chan Kom itself, one sees the emphasis thereby given to the families whose house lots front the plaza. In a bush settlement one house is much like another, and the advantage enjoyed by the owner of a house near the trail that passes through the settlement is not much. But the citizens who own and occupy the houses on the plaza of a pueblo have conspicuous advantage. There is first the relative prestige of their location on the main square. There is the commercial advantage: the plaza is the place to open a store and the place to meet traders. There is the greater frequency of contacts to be experienced by him who lives where visitors and citizens alike come most frequently. It was of course the Tamays, Cemes, and Pats who claimed and obtained house sites on the plaza. No newcomer lives there. Several of the families that have come to Chan Kom since 1931 have at least as much experience with city ways as have the heads of these older families, and they are not poor; but they have had to build their masonry houses on other streets; they are not commonly among those who receive visits and business from the travelers and traders who come to Chan Kom. With the new town plan has come about a corresponding spatial arrangement of the people and of the activities of the town: dominant center and subordinate margins. Also, the continuity of prestige and influence of the leading founding families has been favored.

Some effects of adoption of masonry houses upon the occupants may be suggested if a little imagination be added to observation. One sees that chairs and tables are to be found in many houses in 1948; they were not common in 1931. As possessions usually call for more and related possessions, so masonry houses call for new furniture and bring about some acquaintance with locks and doorknobs. A few houses have not only windows but window screening. The masonry house invites decoration in paint; how painted decorations came to be on the walls of some houses and what is made of them will have mention in following pages. The masonry house is cleaner than an aging house of poles; it is warmer on cold nights—and hotter on hot nights. But those who have masonry houses have not yet come really to live in them. They are not used to eat in, except when meals are served to visitors from town. The masonry house is more easily defended against intruding pigs than is the house of poles, but swine frequently enter stone houses, and little hesitation is shown in storing corn there or in bringing horses through them to the yard in the rear. The kitchen, invariably of poles and thatch, remains the center of the family life; here the women spend most of their time, and here old and young eat, the food handed around, served from the little three-legged table by the fire—the large rectangular table of the towns is not used for the serving of food except on formal occasions or for town visitors. In the kitchen the talk goes on and most of the associating of husbands and wives, parents and children.

There are surely consequences for the people in bringing the houses together in rows along the street, each close to its neighbor on a long lot. It is one of the circumstances that make life noisier, for the voices of one's neighbors and his dogs are now close beside one as one works or sleeps. It brings each resident closely under the possible observation of his immediate neighbors. Among a people who show very great delicacy in avoiding observation and in not observing when one must relieve one's self, in bush or back yard, the new congestion of living must make difficulties. On the whole, people do not peer or exhibit any wish to intrude on one another; one works at what one is doing and does not gaze about.

One probable result is a clearer definition of the paths of activity of the women and perhaps a sharper separation of their usual sphere of activity from that of the men. The wall of façades incloses the women for much of the day behind the street and within the developing patios. There are few paths that cross the walls of the patios; to visit a neighbor, a woman must go out on the street or climb the wall along the patio. While she works, her communication is pretty much restricted to the members of her own household and the neighbors on each side. I do not know whether the women in the bush village take advantage of the more open and casual and generally accessible distribution of houses, unwalled from one another; the woman in the block of masonry houses at least does not have that opportunity. Especially in those cases where the woman may draw water from a well situated within the block on which she lives, she needs go on the street only to take her corn to the mill, and in most cases she has a child to send. Yet it is not to be thought that it is the Moorish seclusion of women which has affected Latin-American ways in Chan Kom; women are retiring and reserved as compared with men, but they are not by them sequestered.

I should not give the impression that in 1948 the people of Chan Kom are living in stone houses. Less than a third of the families have such houses. Most of the members of the households that do have them sleep in the kitchens of poles and thatch. Nor has the advent of the masonry house changed the fact that everyone sleeps in a hammock. No one in Chan Kom has a bed, or a mosquito netting, or a privy. The two shower baths built under teachers' influence have fallen into disuse.

As the community grew, and more and more houses were built at some distance from the plaza, the labor expended in hauling water from the cenote increased. To reduce this labor, and to provide cleaner water, wells were dug. Of the fourteen wells in Chan Kom (and its immediate environs), twelve were dug since 1931. No house in the village is now far from a well, but a few houses at one corner of the plaza are nearer to the cenote than to any well from which the householders are free to draw water, and it is the relatively few women of these houses who still fetch water from the cenote. One well has been built in the center of the plaza; it is used by most of the women whose houses front the plaza, and to it the men bring most of the horses and burros to be watered.

It seems plain that the construction of these wells has tended to divide the community into separateneighbor-hoods. When there were no wells, the cenote was a place to which all the women of the community came. Its edge, under the trees and out of observation because below the level of the houses, was a place to spend a few minutes idling and gossiping. "I heard it at the cenote" was the phrase with which to report a rumor. Today there is no single place to which come all the women. The gristmills, small rooms filled with noisy clatter and with men in attendance, are no substitute. Now the women who meet with one another in the endless task of drawing water are the women of a group of houses that have access to a single well. The prevailing custom of settlement of a married son in a house near that of his father has tended to make the patrilineally related group of families the usual neighborhood. The coming of the well has helped these groups to withdraw each within itself. The conversion of one such patrilineal group to Protestantism was a more important factor in separating that group; this family and another closely associated with it are the families using the cenote. Out in the *colonia* the principal settlement was made by three married brothers; they too have dug a well for themselves and a few neighbors.

The wells were dug under different circumstances of effort and participation and have given rise to different situations of right and to some unresolved problems. In the bush villages, and in the Chan Kom of thirty years ago, important constructions were done by the effort of all residents. Even houses were so built, though enjoyed by a single family. The repair of the curbstones of the cenote, like the clearing of the plaza and the erection of public buildings, are still, naturally, tasks for the entire community to perform. Only the well in the plaza was dug at the common expense; it is recognized as available to all citizens, like the cenote. Three or four of the other wells— among them some of the first wells to be dug—were excavated on street corners for the use of neighbors living at some distance from the cenote. Such wells were built by the joint effort or expense of some of the families that immediately benefited, no effort is made to keep others from using the well, and it is recognized that a well dug on a street belongs to nobody but to everybody. But the other wells have been dug on house lots, and today house lots are private property with title registered under the law of the state. In the cases where only the householder has borne the expense there is no problem, except that of inviting one's neighbors to use the water freely or choosing to try to sell it to them. One man offered to sell a right to use his well for two pesos a month. He found few takers. In each of other cases the well, built by one man on his land, is used, without charge, by his kinsmen who live near him. In one case a group of men, not related, joined to dig a well on the land of one of them. The others feared that one day the landowner would sell his land, when ownership in the well would pass to the purchaser and the informal right they enjoyed in the well be lost. So they built a wall around the well, marking it off from the house lot in an effort—no doubt futile in law—to preserve their rights as against a possible purchaser of the house lot. As such a difficulty is seen, and as wealth increases so that one man alone may dig a well, the tendency is for all future wells to be dug by individual enterprise on private property.

Because they have the money with which to buy them, because they go oftener to the towns where they are sold, and because—probably—the long-run efficiency of a metal vessel is greater than that of a clay one, many metal vessels are in use, and some clay vessels are in disuse. Certain clay vessels used for ceremonial occasions had passed out of use before 1931. The large clay water jug, common then, is now uncommonly seen in the many trips the women make to the wells; as much water is carried in two pails. This involves a change in the use of the body in carrying: traditionally, water jugs, babies, and bundles are carried on the hip (nothing is borne on the head); but two pails cannot be so carried, and women have adopted the almost inevitable way of carrying such containers. Babies are carried as they always were. Nothing has displaced the large wide-mouthed jar for storing water; calabashes are still the common vessel and dipper; and baskets have given little way to wooden chests and wardrobes. The well-to-do and the more town-wise use glass tumblers, china plates and bowls, and metal spoons in greater number and with greater confidence than was the case seventeen years ago, but, so far as we discovered, forks are still unknown.

Since 1938 the women of the village have had the opportunity of bringing their corn to be ground at a motor-driven mill, and since the autumn of 1947 they have had their choice of two mills. I was told that everyone now eats mill-ground corn and found no reason to doubt the statement. The cost is fifteen centavos (three cents) for the grinding of about eight quarts of meal. The consequences of the advent of the mill do not seem to be very far-reaching. In a good many cases some time is freed for the woman of the house, and another errand is to be done by some child of the household. We were told by one concerned with the finer points of cooking that mill-ground corn makes less savory tortillas, but the difference is surely not very significant. The handmill is still used, as when the family must rise early and must first make tortillas to take along to the milpa (though the motor mills are operated at almost any hour, beginning before dawn), and of course the handmill itself is taken along to the milpa with other necessaries when a stay of several days is planned.

In Yucatan—having in mind the state as a whole—the assumption of city dress is significant for the individual in somewhat the same way in which the assumption of the pueblo form is significant for the community. Two kinds of costumes are recognized, and each corresponds to a way of life and, in the city and the towns, to a social class. It is better to say that it did so correspond fifty years ago. At that time the men of the one class wore white shirt and trousers or shorts, sandals, and a round staw hat. The women who shared that life wore the huipil, a wide, waistless embroidered blouse, drew their hair tight back and tied it behind, and went barefoot. Only those men who belonged to the other class and carried on a distinct way of life wore long trousers, often dark, colored shirt with collar, and shoes. Only women of that class wore a dress, usually of some color, and shoes, and dressed their hair in other ways. A wearer of the folk costume was thereby known as a member of the *mestizo* class (whatever his color or racial admixture). A man wearing the folk costume was a manual laborer; certainly he was not a clerk or a streetcar conductor. A woman wearing a huipil might be a domestic servant; surely she was not a trained nurse or an office employee. In the hacienda, and in other rural settlements, the folk costumes were present, clearly to be identified with their corresponding forms in the city, although there were differences, as, for example, in the rural settlements almost all men wore white drawers and an apron of similar length and not long trousers. Men of the upper class—hacienda administrators and merchants —might wear sandals and an all-white costume, but it was notably different from that of the working class. In the rural areas this difference between the one who was *mestizo* and the one who was *de vestido* corresponded also to a difference in "race"; the wearers of the folk costume, laborers in the fields, were Mayas or "mazehua"—Indians—whereas the other kind of people were, to these Maya, "dzulob" (*dzules*), white people, a different kind of people.

These statements are incomplete and do not take account of exceptions. They ignore the relevance, in some situations, of surname, Maya or Spanish, in defining the social position of the individual. Moreover, the changes that are taking place in Chan Kom with regard to costume would not be understood if it were not also made clear that in the last generation or two the *mestizo* costume has come less definitely to serve as an indicator of position in a class or "racial" group. In the city and towns not a few men, and some women, who belonged, or whose fathers belonged, to the lower class, have come to assume the urban costume while still in occupations appropriate to *mestizos*. A more flexible class structure has come into being in which the occupation and the education of the individual has come to count for more in determining his status, and in which those of the lower class have felt freer to give up the folk costume. Nevertheless, in the town or city, where there are the two (principal) classes, and the traditions as well as, in part, the fact of conspicuous difference in costume between them, the giving-up of the folk costume is not lightly accomplished. Each woman who gives up the huipil for the dress makes, as it were, a leap outward and upward; after that she must assume new tastes and powers, while she leaves behind the *jarana* (the dance of the folk) and other ways that are rustic and unsuitable to *mestizas*. The change being difficult for an older person, it is oftenest made by a mother for her daughter, by putting her in a dress early in life or at adolescence. The corresponding change for men is more easily made, for it may be gradually accomplished, adding one garment of the city at a time, perhaps giving up the white drawers for long white or blue-denim trousers before assuming dark trousers and coat. For the man the adoption of shoes in place of sandals is the most significant of these separate changes.

Just in the years that passed between the first observation of Chan Kom and the second its people began an apparent transition from folk to city costume. The significance of the first steps in this transition must be interpreted, however, against the background of the society of Chan Kom itself: its homogeneity and its classlessness.

In 1931 all the people of Chan Kom wore the folk costume, excepting only that a few young men had recently
taken to wearing long trousers, some dark in shade. All the
people had come from communities in which almost everyone wore that costume; the occasional merchant or teacher
who wore the clothing of the city in those communities was
not one of the community; he was, they would say, a *dzul*,
not a Maya.

By 1935 most of the young men had made this change
to long trousers, and one of them, who went often to the
city to buy goods for the store and who had by that time
worked for several months in Merida before returning to
Chan Kom, had brought the complete costume of the city.
The 1940 census reported ninety men as wearing long
trousers and thirty as wearing drawers and apron. In 1948
the original folk costume was worn in its entirety by only
nine or ten of the older men. Moreover, eight men had
bought shoes.

An apparent transition of the women of the community
from the wearing of the huipil to the wearing of dresses
also began in these same years. Unlike the adoption of city
dress by men, the adoption of the dress was in some part
forced. About 1940 the wife of the teacher then in Chan
Kom announced at an evening meeting that all the school
girls would be clothed in dresses and that their hair would
be bobbed, to make them conform with the appearance of
girls in civilized and cultivated communities. From the
little we were told of this, it appears that the reform met
varying response. Some parents co-operated, made the
dresses, and themselves cut their daughter's hair. Others
strongly opposed the change. At a meeting of parents a
decided majority agreed that the change would not be
wise. "If our daughters wear dresses, they will not go to the
milpa. The huipil can stand the wear and tear of the bush;
the dress cannot. And if our daughters wear dresses, who
will marry them? Shall we have to bring down *dzules* from

the city for them?" Such was the sense of words spoken then. Some parents kept their girls home from school.

In 1948 eight or ten teen-age girls wear the dress and one married woman. (In addition, perhaps a dozen little girls wear nondescript dresses.) None have bobbed hair. Of the unmarried wearers of the dress, only two are girls who made the change under the teacher's compulsion or influence; none of the others so affected have maintained the change. Two are younger girls, daughters of that man who makes frequent trips to Merida, who has bought a house site there, and who more than others has devoted himself to the improvement of his family. The other unmarried wearers of the dress are the daughters of one of two newcomers to Chan Kom, one from Kaua, one from a settlement on the highway. The married woman is from Valladolid; she came to Chan Kom *catrina* (as one who wears city clothing is called).

To what extent do these changes of dress represent a transformation that will continue? What are the implications of the change for conduct and attitude?

The adoption of long trousers by the men is more than a change in style of costume over time; it is more consequential than the purely fashionable nylon belts and baseball caps currently worn by youths in 1948. The wearers will not go back to drawers and apron, and these garments, when seen on the men of outlying settlements where they still prevail, appear rustic in the eyes of the younger people of Chan Kom. The assumption of shoes, however, more sharply commits the wearer to identification with the townsman. Of those who bought shoes, two are old enough to have grown children; the others are younger men. To a conservative man, shoes, like the city dress in the case of the woman, tend to separate the wearer from the traditional way of life. Don Eus, who is progressive in his views as to technological improvement and conservative

in his appreciation of the traditional moral life, speaks thus
to his sons: "Shoes and dresses mean being advanced, the
young people say. But I say, then beds follow, and
different foods. One alone can't well go *catrín;* the whole
family has to go. If you go *catrín,* you can't carry a load
on your back, and you aren't content with chayote or
squash. And I say it is ridiculous—then one can't go to a
jarana. And one isn't given free food at fiestas. And it
costs too much money." His sons have not "gone *catrín.*"

But the wearing of dark trousers does not set off the
wearer in any inportant respect from his neighbors who do
not wear them. Both continue to do the same kind of work.
There is no detectable loss in authority or prestige in the
older leader who adheres to the drawers and apron, nor
does he wear these garments with any discoverable embarrassment or sense of apology. The shoes owned in Chan
Kom are seldom worn there; they are chiefly used when
the owners go to town. The new garments have value as
connoting wealth and familiarity with the city, but they
do not, in Chan Kom, relate the wearer to a distinct class
or social group.

From the facts we have it is by no means clear that the
women of Chan Kom are in course of "going *catrín.*" The
efforts of the teacher to bring it about left just two
wearers of the dress. These two, sisters, no longer own any
huipils. If any women of Chan Kom have "gone *catrín,*" it
is these two. But these girls are not yet married. It is
notable that three girls who wore the dress in their school
years and afterward, went back to huipils on their marriage to men of Chan Kom. Just what motivated the
changes is not altogether clear. Every woman can make a
huipil, but only a few can make dresses: this is a circum-
stance favoring the huipil. It is certainly true that many
men in Chan Kom disapprove of the dress, saying that it is
expensive or more often that the wearer of a dress does

not go with her husband to the milpa, nor can she fetch firewood. The girls and the married woman who wear dresses in Chan Kom do not in fact do these things. An outsider may doubt the truth of what men of Chan Kom commonly say to the effect that the dress is impractical for work in the milpa. One sees how easily torn is the long white huipil of light cotton cloth and how much labor is expended in washing that garment; and one imagines a dress of darker color and sturdier material. It is probably more true that the dress keeps the wearer from work in the fields because its connotations with city living make it unsuitable there. In part it is that the girls who adopt dresses have already ceased to fetch firewood. Perhaps, when the girls now wearing dresses come to marry, they will go back to the huipil, as some have already done, in which case the dress will remain for a time, as it is now, an interesting and valued alternative to the huipil, a garment to be worn by young girls who like the change and whose parents provide the dresses. On the other hand, as Chan Kom men marry women from the towns, who have always worn the dress and have lived among women who wear them, it will probably become easier for a Chan Kom married woman to wear dresses. The participation of women in the work of the milpa and in getting firewood will decline; influences from the city rather than forms of costume will carry forward this trend; the change in costume is consistent with it but is not, probably, its necessary cause.

Such facts as we have do not suggest any very sharp separation of meaning between huipil and dress. Except for the two sisters mentioned above, the other teen-age girls who now ordinarily wear dresses also have huipils, and they put these on when they go to the folk dances; the huipil is traditionally appropriate to these *jaranas*. The two women of the community who make women's garments for pay make both huipils and dresses; one wears a dress, the other a huipil. The schoolteacher's daughter, herself no Maya, and of course *catrina*, named four young unmarried girls as the leading ladies of the community; two wearers of dresses, two of huipils. But her more urban viewpoint, as compared with that of the villagers, was represented in her remarks of regret that the second pair did not wear dresses. A girl of the village, fourteen years of age, who wears a dress habitually, said that she liked both huipils and dresses and remarked, without disapproval, that her younger sister wanted a huipil "because they are so pretty."

The fact to be emphasized is that the people of Chan Kom feel themselves to be all one kind of people. They are not divided into social classes. There are not, as we shall see, two racial or cultural groups. The people are sufficiently remote from town and city as not to take part in the class structure of such communities. The difference between Spanish surname and Maya surname in Chan Kom does not signify a difference in social privilege or esteem; the wearer of the dress or of shoes does not make any claim to such advantage. He or she is still the person he or she once was, known to everyone, a Maya, a worker in the milpa or in the kitchen. The dress and the shoe do tend to move the wearers along in the progressive adoption of city ways and city tastes, but they move them only a little and as individuals, separately.

The effect upon the wearer of a dress is probably greatest when the young woman goes to the town or is addressed by some person of the town visiting Chan Kom, for on the whole, in Yucatan, one associates ability to speak Spanish and knowledge of urban ways with the townsman's costume; and, as one is assumed to be, so one tends to become. "Her husband did not want her to put on a dress, because she did not speak Spanish well enough." And Chan Kom people comment unfavorably on the women of a certain little settlement who, though knowing no Spanish, have taken to wearing the dress. Thinking again of the transformation in the houses and town arrangement, one might repeat the observation more generally: Chan Kom, in the last seventeen years, has begun to assume the *persona*, collective and individual, of what Yucatecans know as civilized. The assumption is much more marked in the case of the buildings than it is in the case of the costumes. A representative of the state government, sent down to Chan Kom to conduct some official business having to do with a crime and its punishment, was apparently struck by these evidences of advancement in a region of Indian bush settlement. In comparison with its neighbors, Chan Kom has managed to look "advanced." The visitor was accordingly disposed to accept the account and settlement of the matter provided by the village authorities; these people must know their way about, he felt.

Nevertheless, if one surveys all the "material culture," as anthropologists call it, one sees that much more is unchanged than is changed. The stone houses, china plates, musical instruments, and gasoline or carbide lamps are enjoyed by a minority of families. More than half of the people live in houses and with equipment different in very few particulars from what prevailed a generation ago. And there are many of the tools of living that have changed for no one. Except for the relegation of the hand-mill to a minor place, nothing in the kitchen has undergone any significant change: the same kinds of foods are cooked in the same way on the same sort of fire made on the dirt floor of the house or of an adjacent thatched separate kitchen. Raised plastered stoves were introduced by the mission but are virtually unused. The clothes are washed on the same sort of flat washing board. Everybody sleeps in a hammock. It is the frontispiece of life that has changed: the main streets of the village; the front building, where it is made of masonry, behind which an old-style life goes on in an old-style kitchen; the garb of most men and a few young women. What is behind, inside, more intimate, is much less changed, with regard to the tools and techniques, as also with regard to ideas and attitudes. Yet there are changes in attitudes too that will be discussed later.

III

Commerce, Property, and the Practical Arts

THE bush village is a community with almost no specialization in the practical arts. Every woman does the work of the house, and every man makes milpa, hunts, and builds houses much as does any other. The important specialization that does exist appears in the ritualized or semiritualized work of "the sacred professionals"—the shaman priest, the reciter of prayers, the marriage negotiator, and the midwife. When Chan Kom was first reported in 1931, this situation had not greatly changed. Villa and I wrote: "The secular professionals on whom the people of Chan Kom depend are not themselves people of Chan Kom; they are the merchants, peddlers, professional musicians, migratory artisans and cattle-traders who come to the village or whom the villagers go to find in Valladolid. Among the people of Chan Kom themselves the specialization of secular labor is slight" (pp. 71–72). A baker, a mason who was beginning to teach his art to some of his neighbors, and a barber completed the list of such specialists at that time. The report gave much more space to the ritual and traditional specialists mentioned above.

In these seventeen years Chan Kom has become a community so provided, in its own inhabitants, with artisans and merchants that it now depends little for such services on the towns and that, indeed, the smaller settlements in

its territory have come to depend for them upon it. Chan
Kom has learned how to make much of what it needs and
to get the rest through direct purchase in the city and
resale in the village stores. This accomplishment may be
attributed, in about equal measure, to the initiative of the
Chan Kom people themselves to learn how to do what they
needed to have done and to the efforts of outsiders to teach
the useful arts to the villagers.

The first store in Chan Kom was opened before 1931 by
one of its citizens, but the first store to stock a large
variety of goods was owned and operated by a man of the
towns, one who had come frequently to Chan Kom as a
traveling merchant. After several years this man closed the
store and moved away, but the example he had offered in
merchandising must have affected those in Chan Kom who
opened stores thereafter. Today there are four stores, and
the variety of goods offered is far greater than it was, including occasional delicacies such as cheese and large
oranges brought from outside the village, and flashlights,
baseballs, kitchen knives, and a line of drugs. About half of
the purchasers come from outlying settlements. During the
forty days of our visit in 1948, not one traveling peddler
visited Chan Kom, and apparently they now come very
rarely. Hammocks, however, are still bought in Chan Kom
from traveling vendors who bring them from villages that
specialize in their manufacture.

Bread is baked once a week or oftener by each of two
bakers, and several other men know how to bake and have
built ovens. The first Chan Kom baker learned how to
bake by watching an outsider who was paid to come down
and bake bread in Chan Kom. During the years of
drought (1942–43), five or six Chan Kom men baked
wheat bread steadily to meet the needs of a people de-
prived of corn. Now Chan Kom has become an exporter of
the art as well as of the bread: on two recent occasions men

of the village have gone to neighboring settlements to teach others there—at a fee—the art of breadmaking.

The mason who led in the building of stone houses has moved away, but another, more skilled, has come to Chan Kom, and now not a few of the men know something of this specialty. Carpentry began through the imitation of carpenters who were seen in Valladolid or who came to work in Chan Kom. The cultural mission in 1943–44 very greatly increased the knowledge of this and other arts. One young man was taught to carpenter and still occasionally practices carpentry. Two who were taught leatherwork carry on steadily, in houses that take on the character of workshops and salesrooms, the making of sandals and leather bags. The first wells in Chan Kom were dug by specialists brought in from outside. The mission taught this skill, and seven or eight men of Chan Kom are now available to dig a well for hire. Included in the Mission was a nurse; she taught some of the girls to make hypodermic injections—in Yucatan much medicine is so administered—and they are occasionally called upon to exercise this specialty. Two women have learned, without much formal instruction, the making of dresses and huipils and are employed to make them for others. A desire of the leaders of Chan Kom expressed early in the course of their efforts "to make a pueblo" was the wish to bring music to Chan Kom. They have their wish. In 1937 someone began the teaching of music in the village. About 1940 a family moved to Chan Kom—temporarily—from Merida; the man of the family was a music teacher, and he earned money teaching boys of Chan Kom something about instrumental music. This knowledge was extended by the musician attached to the cultural mission. Today there are two bands in Chan Kom, of brasses, clarinet, and drums, and at least one of these bands is truly professional, for it is employed by neighboring villages to play at fiestas.

If one should suppose that the introduction of new practical arts of life might bring about, or be accompanied by, a decline of more traditional specialties, one would find little in Chan Kom today to support such a conclusion. The twisting of henequen fiber into twine is more rarely seen than it was in 1931. But there are still several families who occasionally make hammocks, some who know how to make baskets, and some—including some of the basketmakers—who make gourd or calabash carriers of palm fiber. This was true in 1931, and at that time, as now, these arts are carried on only occasionally and casually; the articles manufactured are in most cases made for use within the family group.

What is more to be remarked is that the great expansion of specialized handicraft and production for hire, in the arts imported from the town, has not driven out the practitioners of the more esoteric specialties. One might expect the example of the artisan who works for a living and that of the businessman, together with the accompanying influence of urban standards, to reduce the importance of the shaman priest, who carries on a sacred vocation. Indeed, the *h-mens* that once lived in Chan Kom did depart, and in 1935 none lived there. The archaic and sacred profession of the *casamentero*, the elderly man skilful in repeating the formal speeches and in conducting the negotiations incident to an agreement of marriage, was then represented by one elderly man. But these specialties did not disappear from Chan Kom. In recent years a *h-men* has moved to Chan Kom from a small settlement, and several living in neighboring settlements are used by the Chan Kom people. Don Guillermo, who served as *casamentero* in 1931, is an old man in 1948 and spends much time away from Chan Kom; but a new settler is now engaged to help the parents of a boy get the consent of the girl's family. Don Guillermo, who was also *maestro cantor* (reciter and chanter of prayers in the Catholic ritual), has taught his knowledge to a younger man. The woman in Chan Kom who practices herbal medicine, in cases for pay, is frequently called upon. The maintenance of these traditional functionaries implies a persistence of traditional functions and institutions that is indeed the case in Chan Kom and that will receive further attention in these pages.

There are, however, positive consequences of the introduction of the practical arts—with which one may perhaps be justified in including, in this case, instrumental music. The leatherworkers and the principal baker spend so much time at these manufactures that their work in the milpa is much reduced, and they are commonly to be found in their houses and places of business on the plaza. To the extent that these and other men are engaged in handicraft or commerce, they are, for this reason also, taken away from the milpa and are often encountered in their stores and houses. The bush village is without adult male population during most of the daylight hours of the agricultural year. "From the work of the milpa there is no escape," we wrote in 1931. Business and handicrafts, however, are, in part, escapes. And, as already remarked, these activities contribute to the conversion of Chan Kom from a settlement of primitive agriculturalists, depending, so far as it depended at all, on the town and the visiting trader, into a market and manufacturing center. Of course this conversion has not yet occurred: most of the support of Chan Kom is still from agriculture. Nevertheless, within its area, it is now the place to buy most supplies, the place to order sandals, and a source of music for festivals. It may be added that the professionalization of music in Chan Kom has, in one way, made the celebration of festivals less easy, for now if musicians of the village are to be used on such an occasion, they expect to be paid.

One may add an observation that must be in part speculation. The acquisition of new useful techniques that will earn a livelihood inclines cityward the young men who have them. The leatherworker knows that his art is better paid in the city; that there is more demand there for what he knows. One of the local sandalmakers says he is thinking of some day going to the city. He says also that, now he knows how to make sandals, he would like to learn to make shoes. To learn one useful thing and to see what may be gained by its exercise is to begin to think about learning the still more profitable art. And each of the boys who can play a musical instrument with some skill, or who can bake, or dig a well, thinks, one feels sure, that *if* he should go to the city, he would have a means of livelihood. A *milpero* is not wanted in the city. But a good cornet player is.

More striking than acquisition of a number of profitable technical specialties by some of the men of Chan Kom is the great development, in these seventeen years, of livestock industry and of commerce. The two are related. In 1931, we reported, there were "perhaps two score head of cattle" in Chan Kom. In 1935 Steggerda found 168 head of cattle. In 1948 estimates and partial counts showed there were four to five hundred. Hogs have increased almost as rapidly, and the number owned in Chan Kom is very large. The development of livestock industry is general throughout the region, but there are some settlements without cattle—settlements of poor or backward people. The industry developed rapidly in part because the area is relatively free from the epizootics that afflict the western and northern parts of the state.

In 1931 hogs were already a source of revenue; most of them were disposed of by sale to livestock buyers who came down from Valladolid. Cattle, at that time, entered little into commerce. They were a source of prestige and a form for the storage of wealth. Then the owner of a bull thought chiefly of the glory that would attach to him when he entered his animal in one of the rustic bullfights held at the local festivals. Now hog-raising is a principal business of Chan Kom, and cattle-raising is a yet bigger business. One man in 1947 sold cattle to the value of twelve hundred pesos. Also he sold corn to the value of three thousand pesos. Some of the cattle and the corn he raised himself, but some of it he had bought for resale. Many of the more enterprising and experienced men of the village carry on a great deal of this buying and selling.

The advantage the Chan Kom men enjoy over the people in the lesser settlements—the people who have not made their communities into pueblos—lies partly in the exceptional experience of the Chan Kom men in observing the ways of cattle and of cattle-buyers, partly in the position of their community, lying at the center of a web of trails, and partly in the greater amount of money and other capital with which they have to operate. Now they make frequent trips to settlements in the area, buying hogs, cattle, or corn and bringing them to Chan Kom to raise for market. They own horses with which they can transport the corn and, if need be, the hogs. They hold what they have bought for a favorable market, and one or two of them read newspapers for market information. Men who seventeen years ago would have been working only in their milpas today, instead, are busy making these trips or receiving corn as it comes in small quantities to their houses or stores. A characteristic transaction may be described: A Chan Kom storekeeper sold to a man of Xanla (a smaller and more isolated settlement) soap, salt, and other staples for twenty-five pesos, delivering the goods to him in Xanla. The Xanla man had a small store but no horse. While in Xanla, the Chan Kom man bought four *cargas* (loads) of corn at 6.50 pesos a *carga*. He made a profit of three pesos on the sale of the staples, and later sold the corn at Chichen Itza at nine pesos a *carga*. In the following week the same man made a profit of fifty pesos by purchase and quick resale of hogs.

This sort of business is carried on by men who do not think of themselves as merchants and who pursue such activities in a casual and irregular way. But nine or ten of the men of Chan Kom are in the full sense commercial men, for they steadily and regularly devote themselves to buying and selling, and they buy and sell in large quantities. The principal business of these men is in hogs, with cattle and corn secondary. They make much more extended trips, going into the remoter hinterlands to find livestock; they have arrangements with truck-owners to meet them at Chichen and from there to transport their purchases to Merida; and they enter into partnerships, at least for each trip or unit of enterprise, with other men, for hog-drovers must work in pairs or in groups. These men have assumed all the functions which were performed in 1917 only by men from the towns; then Chan Kom was merely one of the little settlements to which came buyers from the towns in the hope of buying there a hog or two. Furthermore, Chan Kom is becoming a sort of station or depot in the swine trade. The improvement of trails to Chan Kom brings hog-drivers through the village who turn out of their direct route to drive their hogs by the broader trails that pass through Chan Kom and who often pass a night, or the hot midday hours, in the village.

The origins of this development of cattle industry and of commerce are to be found, as already indicated, in the exploitation by Chan Kom people of the relative advantage they early gained over neighboring settlements. They have developed their wealth into more wealth, and they have profited by their greater opportunities to learn from the foreign cattle-buyers and hog-drovers. It is also true that the development of commerce in a growing community so situated as is Chan Kom is not only an opportunity but a necessity. This follows from the pressure of population on limited resources in land. When the Spaniards introduced and compelled concentration of Indian populations into towns, they made commerce and manufacture inevitable, if the towns were to continue. The engineer who surveyed the Chan Kom lands in 1925 described them as "rugged and very stony." This, indeed, they are. In only a few places in the communal lands are there patches of deeper, moister soils. The lands are on the whole such that they will yield a harvest only of corn or beans, and these may be planted in any one tract for only two or at most three years before the land must be allowed again to return to bush and remain scrub forest for about ten years.

So long as there remained to the south an unpopulated territory, it was possible to take care of the increasing numbers of people by the making of new settlements on that frontier. The people of a village would go farther and farther from their home community to find good land. Thus would develop temporary settlements of agriculturalists, at home in a parent-community but spending much time at the distant *milperío*. In time the connections with the home community would become irksome, and the *milperío* would become a new and independent center of settlement. Thus it was that Chan Kom itself came into being. So long as Chan Kom remained small, it could continue as an agricultural settlement. But its decision to become a pueblo, and so to become larger, made it increasingly difficult for the people to sustain themselves on the land. *Ejidos* were formally assigned to Chan Kom, but it has already been explained that this event did not really increase the resources of the village, for before the government got around to regularizing the rights as to land in that part of the state, and when the population there was sparse, the Chan Kom people made milpa almost where they wished.

Furthermore, there is good reason to suppose that the lands available to the village yield less than they did twenty-five years ago. There can be no doubt but that sugar, a significant crop thirty years ago, is now grown nowhere by Chan Kom people. Pineapples have almost disappeared. The people of Chan Kom mention now two or three places only where "good land" is available to them. Beans, sweet potatoes, yams, squash, *jícama*, and chile are still planted, but the general report is that the yields are smaller. The same report is given as to corn. In 1931 we found that the average yield of corn per *mecate* (about one twenty-fifth of a hectare) was 0.8 of a *carga* (a *carga* is about 42 kilos). For the years 1932–34 Steggerda obtained figures indicating an average yield of about 0.65 of a *carga*; 1934 was a very bad year. The men who gave opinions to me in 1948 said that now the average yield is about half a *carga*. I have not investigated the causes of this reduction in average yield. The people feel sure that the land is less productive. The rapid destruction of the large trees, with perhaps soil erosion, may be a factor. It may also be true that, as land becomes scarcer, it is planted again in a shorter interval after its last abandonment to bush.

So Chan Kom may and must supplement its agriculture with other means of support. The average size of milpas is surely smaller now. Five of the leading citizens, who are all engaged in commerce in one way or another, said that they are planting milpas about one-half as large as they used to plant. A leading hog-buyer plants just enough land to provide his family with corn; this is the extent of corn-raising done by a principal storekeeper and operator of three gristmills (two in other villages). It is important to note that we could find no one who has given up the making of milpa altogether. The making of milpa is so central a part of the traditional activities of the people, still so closely attended with moral and religious sanctions, that for these reasons it would be hard entirely to abandon. And I think that a feeling of insecurity comes to that man who makes no milpa even if he has money with which to buy his maize. Certain it is that with prosperity the people of Chan Kom, though they reduce the amount of land planted in maize, on the average, do not reduce, but rather increase, the store of maize in their granaries. This they do, of course, by buying maize when the price is low. "There is now in Chan Kom enough maize to feed the people for three years," I was told. More and more of the time and efforts of the men go into raising livestock, into buying and selling, and a little manufacturing. They increasingly profit, too, from the agricultural efforts of others and, purchasing the fruits of the labor of men of other settlements, provide their own stores of grain.

The wealth of Chan Kom, so greatly increased in these seventeen years, is chiefly kept in liquid capital. It is put into cattle, hogs, maize, and the gold chains that women wear with their fine huipils and that are traditionally forms of storage of wealth. Probably the wealthier men keep hundreds of pesos, or even a thousand or more in the form of cash. There is no banking, and the money is simply put away in the village. The expenditure of money on musical instruments, better clothing, and other consumption goods is notable, but it surely does not absorb a large part of the new wealth.

The accumulating wealth, the disappearance of the open frontier, and the successful efforts of the state and federal governments to bring rights in land into conformity with law—with certain other circumstances soon to be noted—bring about a much greater emphasis upon individual property rights. Land not granted to villages as *ejidos* has become available for sale as land titles have been regularized, so that in recent years a number of the wealthier men of Chan Kom have bought land outside the *ejidos*. One has bought a tract including three thousand *mecates;* he will have the title registered. It is his plan to divide this land among his sons, so each will be provided for.

As yet this acquisition of large private estates in land is confined to a few men. Others, however, are developing limited private land within the *ejidos*. This is possible through a modification made in recent years in the law as to communal village property, which, I am told, provides that every shareholder (*ejidatario*) in the communal land may receive from the government a certificate establishing his exclusive right to a certain parcel of land within the *ejido*, subject to the condition that within two years from the granting of the certificate the holder works the land and continues to work it for two years. The right is not ownership, for the *ejidatario* may not sell the land. He may, however, transmit his right to his son. No one may hold more than one parcel of such land, and one must work the land personally. Women may have such parcels (must they also work the land personally?), but a woman who has such a parcel loses her right to it when she marries a man who has a parcel. These, at least, are the principal provisions of the law as they are understood by the men of Chan Kom who spoke of it to me and as they appear on an official announcement.

Four or five of the men have begun the development of such small tracts by planting fruit trees, tomatoes, beans, and other small crops, by building cattle corrals, establishing poultry on the tract, and, in a few cases, by digging wells. The tracts so far so developed are from four hundred to six hundred *mecates* in size. When these enterprising men first began these developments—before, indeed, the law was made known—they were opposed by some in the village who felt that these rural developers would somehow come to own the tracts outright and sell them, thus profiting from communal lands at the expense of other holders of rights therein. And though this cannot happen, as the new law comes to be understood and accepted, its application contributes to the growing emphasis on private rights, for the man who develops such a tract comes to feel it is as good as his own; it is quite different from the milpa which goes back to bush after a few years of cultivation and so never becomes anyone's land. These little rural properties are qualified assignments to individuals of exclusive rights in certain property. In each such tract, though as yet there are few of them, the agriculturalist makes an investment for the indefinite future.

A development of exclusive individual right in the house lots of the village has also taken place in these years. In 1931 it was recognized by law and by custom that the man who received a lot marked out to lie along a street on which he would build his house received only a right of use of the lot which he would forfeit should he leave the village to go to live elsewhere. Nevertheless, at that time, the man who built a house or made other improvements on a house site felt that he should be allowed to sell the lot or at least the house and to pocket the proceeds, and indeed the village authorities were then beginning to allow the retiring owner to sell the house and lot, provided he sold it to some resident, old or new, of Chan Kom. The building of masonry houses, so much greater an investment than are houses of poles and thatch, contributed to the development of this feeling for ownership in the house lot. In 1948 the law of the state apparently gives recognition to full individual ownership of house lots, for title to them is now registered in the city, and the owners are provided with documents of title. The people too now fully support the intentions of the law; it is taken as a matter of course that a man who has received a lot from the village authorities owns the lot and may sell it to whomever he wishes, whether or not the purchaser resides or comes to reside in Chan Kom. And this is true even though, as is the practice, the newcomer to Chan Kom receives a house lot without cost. He pays for it, as the people feel, in the labor which he performs, as a citizen, on public improvements.

Thus the public opinion of Chan Kom and the law that is now enforced there have come to support individual rights in almost all sorts of land. In the bush village which Chan Kom once was almost no land was individually owned. A man went into the bush and made milpa where the land appeared suitable and where no one else was then making milpa. Even the boundaries of the land "belonging" to other settlements were uncertain. In the village a man, too, built his house in any unoccupied spot, and his neighbors helped him build it. When he left, someone else occupied the house, or it fell apart. If fruit trees or other plantings were made, they were in most cases made in the milpa or near the planter's house, and it was understood that the planter owned the tree, whoever might claim a right to the land. In 1931 ownership of fruit trees on another's land was still recognized. But in 1948 people are not planting fruit trees except on land which they own, and, as has already been described, they are coming to dig their wells each by his separate effort or expenditure on his own individual property. Much of the land outside the *ejidos* is now recognized as owned by individuals, and the house sites are owned and freely sold. The streets, plaza, cenote, and wells dug in the streets are of course recognized as common property. The *ejido* remains a tract of land for agricultural use of which the village as a whole is the owner, but it is coming to be divided into separate tracts which each owner exploits through the years to his own exclusive advantage.

The vastly increased commerce and the rapid development of recognition of individual property rights are changes received with satisfaction by the men of Chan Kom with whom I spoke. I heard no objection to either trend, except in so far as I was told that for a time some people resented the exploitation of tracts of land within the *ejido* by the few enterprising developers of these tracts; and the present law on this subject is apparently respected. The vastly increased commerce is applauded. The people speak pridefully of the frequency with which dusty droves of hogs pass through the plaza. "Now there is much activity." They like to see twenty swine penned in a village corral, ready for market; and the many cattle that cross the plaza to the central well to be watered are good to look upon. The bush around the village teems with cattle and hogs. So too is the emphasis on individual property rights strongly approved. The *ejidos* were granted to the village with the national policy that they be held in common by all the agriculturalists of the village, and at the time of the grant the people thought of their lands as the lands to which the community belonged, to be enjoyed by all, by grace of the supernaturals. Now the people approve of the recognition of individual rights in the *ejidos*. "Now there is no communism; property is respected." The men of Chan Kom regard the respect for property as a foundation of society. The increase of cattle and the growing density of population contribute to the frequency with which trespasses upon milpas by cattle take place. This is an old problem, now more difficult. There is an inevitable basis for conflict between that backward settlement that depends solely on its plantings of corn, and the owner, in another settlement, of cattle that roam far. Deer are growing scarce, and meat is hard to come by. When the cattle of the other settlement, perhaps a settlement hated for its power and success, break into a milpa and eat a man's corn, what is a man likely to do? In

1948 four men of such a backward settlement were arrested and brought to Chan Kom and there convicted, on their confessions, of killing for meat the cow of a well-to-do resident of another settlement. The conviction of these miscreants and their removal to the penitentiary in Merida were received with immense satisfaction. When a representative of city authority told the people that Mexican law permitted the owner of a cow or a sack of corn to shoot, and to kill, a thief caught in the act, this information passed rapidly from one to another—and was received with expressions of high approval. "Now property is respected."

Would better knowledge than we have of the poorer men of Chan Kom show a different attitude? Perhaps, but I doubt it. There are not many who are very poor. There is a widow who lives on charity and by the performance of small tasks of service. She had plenty of money once. There are some men who came to Chan Kom destitute during the famine years of 1942–43; so far as we know they have all made good new beginnings toward economic security in Chan Kom. Five or six men have once or twice gone to work in a sawmill about seventy-five miles away and in a coconut plantation near the coast; these men continued to make milpa in Chan Kom and took the distant employment in the slack season of agriculture. One man, said to be the poorest in Chan Kom, went off and spent a long season collecting chicle in Quintana Roo but apparently came back as poor as he went. He and his family share a small house with a friend's family. The increase of wealth has no doubt increased the difference in wealth between the richest man of Chan Kom and the poorest man. But there is no group of the known and self-known poor. With industry and fair luck anyone can still get along in Chan Kom. Those who want to employ labor to do the work of the milpa or to build walls have great

difficulty in finding anyone who will take the employment
—and money wages have increased with the cost of
commodities.

The development of commerce has surely provided new
sources of conflict within Chan Kom itself, or it serves to
aggravate old ones. In the bush village every man started
more or less even with any other and went out into a land
of open resources to make his living. His success followed
from his industry (and his piety, the people would say).
What he gained did not, in any direct way, take away from
his neighbor. Even in a larger community, with more
limited resources, this situation prevails so long as everyone is an agriculturalist and most of the land must go
back to nature and, one might say, the general public,
every few years. It prevailed in Chan Kom in 1931. But
when villagers are engaged in commerce, under each
other's noses, and compete for trade, the situation is
plainly different. The subgroups of these Yucatecan villages and the anciently and persistingly competitive
groups are the patrilineal great families. If these families
more or less co-operate for the common good, the village
prospers. If they engage in bitter struggles with one another, the village cannot go forward. When an outsider, a
new inhabitant, set up a gristmill in Chan Kom, unconnected with the principal families, it was a public service.
When he sold the mill to the head of one of these families,
and when, later, another family set up another mill, then
everyone in the village could see who took her corn to
whose mill. Of the four existing stores, one each of three
belongs to a representative, respectively, of the Ceme,
Tamay, and Pat families. We were not able to prove the
following, but observations made strongly suggest it: the
citizen whose loyalties are notoriously committed to one
of these families is apt to buy his goods at that store; the
citizen who "doesn't want to mix in such disputes" will

take care to patronize each on occasion; yet anyone, almost, will go to a store where he can buy something he needs that is not to be had at the others.

These three stores are private enterprises for profit. The fourth store has been organized under the law which provides for co-operative retail stores. By this law such a store is freed from the payment of taxes which other stores must pay but is subject to certain limitations: it cannot charge more than a limited amount over cost; it may not sell liquor; it must make periodic reports to state authority. Such a store is to benefit its community by controlling exploitation by individual merchants. The law requires that at least ten persons sign the papers of organization and constitute the co-operative. In the case of the Chan Kom store all ten were found among the members of one of the three principal families. It is not surprising that it is not fully regarded as a community enterprise. The municipal president of Chan Kom in office not long ago was the owner of one of the other stores. As municipal president it was his duty to collect taxes from all private village stores. The co-operative paid no taxes. But was it a co-operative? The mill, the mill which was not the one to which the municipal president's wife took her corn, was included in the co-operative. And so the mill paid no taxes. Under the influence of drink (an uncommon influence in Chan Kom), the bitterness that this situation engendered burst forth one day. It burst forth out of a rancor that simmers from time to time in the buying and selling of hogs and cattle at quick profit, out of the mills that by their noise announce the business they take in on opposite sides of the plaza, out of the four stores, out of the maize that used to be chiefly food and the fruit of labor and piety and that is now also something to amass and hold for a favorable market.

Chan Kom has commerce. Is it characterized by commercialism? In 1927 Villa found a people whose interest in prices was limited to the prices of the few commodities they bought or sold: corn, hogs, cotton cloth, machetes. The contacts soon thereafter with Chichen increased their acquaintance with money values, and fowl, eggs, and fruit came to be priced and sold, yet their conceptions as to incomes received by the people of the city were fantastic, and their economy was still related to that of the outside world in terms of only a few common pecuniary values. Within the community few prices were made. In 1931 I wrote: "Months may go by without a sale of cattle"; and when I came to the village I was received as a guest; with some difficulty I arranged to pay for at least the food that was provided me from the one little store. Villa remembers that in that same year there was some discussion as to whether the men of the village who organized the patronal festival should continue, as was customary, to provide food free to all visitors, and the example of the city, in selling a plate of beans for twenty-five centavos, was cited. In 1935 a man of the village sold Villa an archeological relic; in other cases at this time such transfers were by gift only.

Chan Kom is surely far more familiar with prices, and more at ease in making money transactions, now than it was then. In these seventeen years the people have received many visitors and have come to take it as a matter of course that serving a meal will bring money and that house rent be paid by one who is given lodging. The price of an article one sees in another's possession is asked more freely now than it was before. In 1931 such loans as were made did not bear interest. In 1948 we found it common to lend money, sometimes in large amounts, apparently usually with a written receipt given; if the borrower is not a close friend or relative, it is likely that interest will be asked. The two or three women who "take in washing" have fixed prices for each article or service. I was told that although "in the early days" a woman of Ebtun might go to Valladolid and there obtain employment as a house servant, those widows who support themselves in Chan Kom today in part by performing these needed services for pay are a new phenomenon. For what the evidence may be worth, it may be added that, although the midwife who practiced in Chan Kom in 1931 charged a traditional fixed fee for bringing a baby into the world, the midwife who practices there today charges from five to twenty-five pesos, depending on the difficulty of the birth, the length of the journeys she has to make, and her personal relationships to her patients.

These employed women are, however, exceptional in Chan Kom. The men of Chan Kom exhibit that much greater familiarity with prices and judging what is pecuniarily profitable that is to be expected from their much greater experience with buying and selling. The embroidery of tablecloths and garments is an old art among the women. It has had no commercial exploitation locally, and the makers of such articles are at a loss as to how to fix a price at which to sell them. It was a difficulty, an embarrassment, for the woman whom we employed to do domestic work during our stay in the village in 1948 to accept money from us; she would have felt easier if she could have done it in exchange for some service from us or for reasons of personal liking and confidence. In spite of the growing familiarity with money transactions, there are even more transactions by way of gift—honey, or sweet potatoes, or oranges, handed over the house-lot wall to a friend, a neighbor, a *compadre* who accepts, pleased—feeling he must some time reciprocate.

The people of the village have taken to commerce both with outsiders and among themselves. But commercialism has not, to our knowledge, entered the primary family,

nor has it attached itself to religion and festivals. No
case was discovered of sisters, or brothers living together,
doing business of any importance with each other or of a
father hiring his son—or a son his father. The fiesta of
San Diego, the patron, and the fiesta of the Holy Cross
do not bring out vendors or other commercial enterprise.
Yucatan has long been without local markets of native
products, nor is there any indication that they are developing in the region in which Chan Kom lies. Business expands, but it expands in the sphere of business. Nor is the
care of money a developed concern. It surprised us to see,
in many cases, how casually coins and bills were left
around—in old tin cans on a shelf, behind bottles in a
store, or tucked up among burlap sacks. Money is sent
from settlement to settlement in little paper wrappings, by
persons who happen to be going that way. This is honesty,
one says. Also it represents a lack of emphasis on the
symbols of the pecuniary life.

IV

The Stability of the Social Organization

IN 1920 Chan Kom, like other folk societies, was composed of people all very similar in appearance, habit, and view of life. Like other such communities too, it conducted its affairs chiefly by the exercise of those diffuse controls which depend on personal relationships and are expressed in conversation, gesture, and ceremony. It was a community of people who had little to do with outsiders. The whole village was a single neighborhood made up of intermarried families. These statements could also be made of Chan Kom in 1931, with the additional statement that by that time, when the community was first studied, a simple but more formal structure of government, in the offices appropriate to a village recognized by the state and federal governments, had been added. Then, in the following seventeen years, many events occurred which might be expected to modify the simplicity of the social organization and of the mechanisms of social control: a growth in population; a great increase in communication, transportation, and commerce; and the achievement of the political status of a "free municipality." The extent and the nature of these modifications are the subject of this chapter.

In the seventeen years that elapsed between the two studies of the village, its population increased by almost three-fourths. Most of the increase—three-fifths—came in the last eight years. From accounts given, there were not more than twenty-five people living around the cenote in

67

1905; not more than one hundred in 1910. The population (217) claimed by the people of the village in 1923, when they filed their petition for grant of *ejidos* was almost certainly an exaggeration; it was one commonly made under such circumstances. The national census in 1930 was made in the village by Villa, then schoolteacher; it showed 251 inhabitants. In 1935 Steggerda counted 244. The decrease was probably real: this was the period in which severely arduous collective labor was required by the village authorities of all citizens in accomplishing public works, and on this account several families left the village; there was as yet nothing much in Chan Kom to attract new residents. The national census made in 1940 reported 270 inhabitants. The count we made in 1948 showed 437 inhabitants. The figure is too low rather than too high, as a number of infants escape the knowledge of the enumerator. A second and more careful count of ten households showed that one recently born inhabitant had been overlooked on the first visit. Perhaps, then, there are 445 inhabitants in Chan Kom today. On the other hand, this number is greater than the number of people who are actually staying in Chan Kom in any one night, for there are always families away, at their milpas or elsewhere. The composition of the population according to age shows no significant change as the census of 1930 is compared with that of 1940: in the latter year it was still true that about three-fifths of the inhabitants were under five years of age and about one-fourteenth of them over forty-five years of age. Unless verified by birth records, information as to age in Chan Kom is very unreliable. We made no attempt to record ages in the census we made in 1948.

The increase in population has of course resulted from a combination of additions to the population and of withdrawals from it—by emigration as well as by death—which has affected, positively or negatively, the homogeneity of the people. The departures of certain families in the years from 1930 to 1935 increased the homogeneity. At that time the leaders insisted with zeal and firmness on the building of school and roads, and those citizens who had little taste for making progress at such a cost withdrew to other settlements. Moreover, when the first stone school building collapsed and killed a member of the Caamal family, several other families of related Caamals promptly moved away. The people who remained were those who had the heart for stern effort. Then, when in these same years a number of families were converted to Protestantism and wide differences thus developed within the community, upon the decision of the majority to return to Catholicism, several of the Protestant families left Chan Kom. So the leadership of the community, the predominating policy, works selectively upon the changes of population by migration so as to bring about a population of similar people. On the other hand, the new customs and the new contacts tend to bring about diversity among the people. After 1940, when the effects of the success of Chan Kom in becoming the paramount community of its territory were beginning to be felt, the greatest influx of new settlers occurred. They came because Chan Kom was the place where there were stores, wealth, music, and lights, or because after the severe drought in 1942-43 they had to make a new beginning somewhere.

A comparison of the composition of the population in 1931 with that of the population in 1948 will show the extent to which the community has become heterogeneous or has changed in its origins or its education and past experience. The situation in 1931 may be first considered. Information was obtained as to the pueblos of origin of sixty-three of the approximately one hundred family heads (husbands and wives) then in Chan Kom. Of these sixty-three, sixty had come from villages, predominately or exclusively

Maya, small in size, and within fifty miles of Chan Kom. The other three had come from larger and more hispanified and modified towns; one woman was from Merida. If the Ceme family be included—and it might well be, for although its pueblo of origin was regarded as Pixoy, the family heads had moved to Ebtun when the people later to come to Chan Kom were yet children—then thirty-eight of the sixty-three were from the "parent-village" of Ebtun; these included the Ceme, Pat, Tamay, and Caamal families. Additional information as to the remaining two-score family heads would not much change this view of the uniformity of the population, as to cultural antecedents, in 1931.

In 1948 what has become of the fifty families that had made up Chan Kom in 1931, and what is the character of the families that have come to settle there in the interval and who have remained?

Information was obtained in 1948 as to forty-two of the fifty families of 1931. Five families had disappeared through death of both of the couple or through death of one with absorption of the survivor into the household of a child or other relative. Sixteen families had moved away. Twenty-one of forty-two of the 1931 families were still present in 1948, headed by one or both of the spouses who headed them in 1931. In 1948 there are seventy-three family households in Chan Kom. Twenty-seven are households established by a son of one of these "old settlers," or by a brother, unmarried in 1931. Twenty-five are headed by new residents who have moved into Chan Kom since 1931. And the remaining twenty-one households—making up the seventy-three families of the present—are the surviving "original" families who were already there in 1931.

Thus two-thirds of the family households of the Chan Kom of 1948 are the households that were there in 1931 or are offsprings of such. The degree of persistence of the "original" families is even greater, for, of the twenty-four married men who have moved into Chan Kom since 1931 and stayed there, nine have married daughters of "original" settlers. (Fifteen have brought wives from elsewhere.) In nineteen of the seventy-three family households of Chan Kom today one or the other spouse is a Ceme. The Tamays also remain in numbers and in influence. The Pat great family is the principal family to become Protestant, and many of its family households have moved away.

As to all but one of the "new families," we learned something dependable as to their pueblos of origin—at least as to the communities from which they moved to Chan Kom. Eighteen of these twenty-three new settlers come from settlements no larger than is Chan Kom at present, settlements of people wholly or very predominantly Maya, settlements of simple agriculturalists. About half came from very small settlements—*rancherías* or *milperíos*. So there are only five families, of the seventy-three in Chan Kom, that provide or that might be thought to provide new elements of civilization or of sophistication to the community. Two of these families came from Noh Itza, a small settlement but one which has easy access to the road to Merida on which the busses run and in which the people speak Spanish, not Maya, as the language of ordinary use. So now there are two families in Chan Kom where Maya is not spoken; this is a novelty. One new settler is from Xocempich, a slightly more sophisticated but quite Maya community—a community in which the Protestant mission for the state has its headquarters. But the newcomer to Chan Kom from Xocempich is a *h-men*, a man as characteristic of the old culture as one would find. The remaining two came from Dzitas, a considerably more sophisticated community, a railroad terminus. One of these two is a simple Maya agriculturalist. The other gave up his residence in Chan Kom while we were there in 1948, taking with him to Merida, as his accepted spouse, the daughter of an old settler.

Only one of the Chan Kom men has taken a wife from a town, and he has done so twice. The first marriage was with a woman of Merida who came temporarily with her family to Chan Kom; she had a Maya surname but was much more citified than the young man; the marriage soon ended in divorce. The second wife is from Valladolid; she is the one married woman who dresses *catrina*, and her house shows some of the amenities or little forms of town life; the difference between this and that of any of its neighbors is not great, however.

The result of this survey is that there is not yet any resident of Chan Kom, any full participator in the community (for teachers and missionaries and ethnologists are but visitors), who has a way of life notably different from that of the rural agricultural Maya settlement. The statement made, one must report one very apparent but ineffective exception and one impending important exception. The important exception—if it comes to pass—would result from the marriage, now under private discussion by the parties and by everybody else, of a city girl, daughter of a schoolteacher, with one of the Spanish-speaking and better-schooled youths. As this girl's mode of life and manner is notably different from that of the native women, manual workers with little freedom of speech and manner, her entrance into the village life, should she come there and remain, might be a significant event. The other possible exception exists in the person of an old man, yet vigorous, from the interior of the Republic, a "Mexican" as contrasted with "Yucatecans." This man has lived in Chan Kom for several years, occupying alone a thatched house vacated by a settler who moved away and buying his food from neighbors. He speaks no Maya and looks and in manner acts quite differently from the Maya. He is conspicuously different, as one sees him go about, briskly, wearing a wide Mexican hat. Nothing need be written here about this man except that he is fully accepted by the people as a citizen with rights and obligations like any other settler and that he apparently influences them very little. He makes milpa, chats in the store with those who speak Spanish, keeps out of controversy and local politics, and in no way we could discover is a source of change in the life of Chan Kom.

The people of Chan Kom are, then, still all the same kind of people, with slight exception. And they strongly feel themselves to be all the same kind of people. In 1948, as in 1931, they think of themselves as Maya, *mazehua*, as contrasted with *dzules*, white people, people of the city. If anything, the disposition to include every enrolled citizen of the village among those who are Mayas is greater now than formerly, for the same men who in 1931 told me that certain residents at that time who had Spanish surnames were, on this evidence, not fully Maya, but "mixed Maya" or "half Maya," in 1948 insisted that the few individuals living in the village with Spanish surnames were just as Maya as the others. "They are Maya because they live just as we do. They can go into the bush, and work hard there." So even the woman from Valladolid, who wears a dress, and has a Spanish surname, is regarded as fully Maya. Another woman, with Maya surname, who has lived for years in Merida, has never lived in a small village, and who has the manners of the town (but who wears a huipil) was also unhesitatingly regarded as Maya. The case of the Mexican made difficulty for Don Eus Ceme: this man does not speak Maya, does not look like a Maya, and is known to come from afar; yet, as he made milpa and lived by hard work among the villagers in the manner of the villagers, Don Eus could not call him a *dzul*. He could not, because a *dzul* is a softer, town-inhabiting creature. After some hesitation he suggested that perhaps there were some Mayas in other parts of Mexico from whom this man had descended.

Only the teacher, his wife and daughter—and the visiting ethnologists—were recognized as *dzules* among those in Chan Kom. Accordingly the idea of marriage between a teacher's daughter and a boy of the village was regarded as an undesirable and probably unsuccessful match. To Don Eus, the Mayas and the *dzules* are two different "races," and he compares them with East Indian cattle and "native" cattle, or with different breeds of fowl. As he regards crosses of such breeds as probably undesirable, so he regards intermarriage of the two human races as undesirable. Yet he does not identify the *dzul* and the Maya by their physical appearance. "One can be very light in color and still be a Maya." On the other hand, people entirely Indian in physical appearance may be *dzules*. It is the mode of life that chiefly persuades him that an individual is a Maya; the Maya surname is additional but not needed evidence. If a person who lives entirely as a *dzul*, in the city, has a Maya surname, then he too is really a Maya, one who has learned to live as the *dzules* do. This account certainly lacks something in internal consistency, but it represents the view of Don Eus; and conversations with other men in Chan Kom show that others look at the matter in the same way.

The people of the village have, then, no less consciousness than they had in 1931 that they are Indians, a people different from the urban people; and they may indeed feel that difference more strongly than they did at that time. On the other hand, they are plainly now more at home with the *dzules*. They see many more of them. Far more frequently than in 1931 do they go to Chichen and to Merida. The hog merchants of Chan Kom, who as such did not exist in 1931, today make their trips for buying and selling in company with men of the towns, and they deal with *dzules* when they hire their trucks and when they sell their swine. Several families in Chan Kom now have close relatives who live in Merida, and commonly they stay in their houses, among *dzules*, when they make their not infrequent visits to the city. And *dzules* come more commonly to the village. The visits of the hog-drovers who pass through the village, the coming of officials required to come to Chan Kom now that it is the head of a *municipio*, the long experience the villagers have had with investigators of the Carnegie Institution, the residence in the community for a year and a half of the ten *dzules* making up the cultural mission, and protracted visits of as many missionaries of the evangelical Protestant religion—all these events have made the presence of *dzules*, for purposes understood and accepted, frequent in Chan Kom. So the *dzul* is now treated as a commonplace. In 1931 it was a matter of general interest and importance that a "distinguished visitor" should be received by the village. On the occasion of many a visit made to Chan Kom in the 1930's, especially by Americans, people came out of their houses, each to make his little expression of welcome, with a gesture of handshaking or a gift of flowers. Some such visits were honored with ceremonial dinners with speeches or with *jaranas*. Then the *dzules* were not only novel: they were needed by Chan Kom in its ambitions to become an important pueblo, a civilized community. Now the ambition is realized. Now the people have passed through twenty years of improving and reforming and investigating visits by *dzules*. There is no lack of friendliness toward the urban visitor now, but there is much less interest in him. Only personal friends come out to greet a visitor. The official or the merchant who comes to Chan Kom does his business, lingers a little while, and departs; only those with whom his business causes him to deal take any part in the recognition of his coming or going. Other people may watch from their doorways, but they do not step forward. Chan Kom has become incorporated into the political and economic world of the city: ceremonies of meeting between the village world and the city world are therefore no longer needed.

The significant differences, as between one individual and another, are, then, first, the difference between a Maya and a *dzul* and, second, the difference between a citizen and patriot of the village—a person of Chan Kom—and one whose residence and loyalties belong to some other community. These are categories that have long been emphasized, and no great change has occurred with regard to them in these seventeen years.

Nor has there come about any development of social classes within Chan Kom. The words written about the village in 1931 on this point might stand to describe the situation in 1948: "There are no social classes. . . . Differences in status are not conferred by birth; some families are more powerful than others because the individuals separately enjoy status and because they co-operate with one another; but social superiority is not conferred by one surname rather than another. Nor are any prerogatives transmitted by inheritance or succession." It is true that the differences between one individual or family and another with regard to either wealth or acquaintance with the city are somewhat greater now than they were in 1931, but now, as then, "there are no terms to describe such differences in sophistication within the community and no differences in costume or occupation that might symbolize such differences in status." A man may be described as "rich" or as "having property," but we heard no reference, with respect to the villagers, to "the rich" or "the poor." That the assumption of city costume does not identify the wearer with any distinguished or named group has already been declared. There is no term that groups together people of the village who carry on a way of life more urban, more "sophisticated," than that of contrasted people. People do not refer to "the merchants" or "the shopkeepers." It is simply that Gabino makes sandals, and Maximo knows how to carpenter; there are the Tamay store and the Pat store. The sense of alikeness among the villagers is strong and is not yet qualified by recognition of occupational or status groups.

Examination of the conduct that underlies the use of terms and the sense of alikeness does not much change this understanding of the situation. Men do respect and put confidence in those who have cattle and other wealth. These are the men to whom money may be safely lent, and these are the men who ought to maintain control of the public affairs of the village. Mention has been made of the recent tendency for neighborhood groups to form; a small informal gathering with phonograph music in a private house may draw neighbors together, but not the whole community. Except for this, and except as family or religion enters in—matters which will be discussed below—there seems to be no tendency for part of the population to associate together as against some other part. At any rate, there is no tendency to exclusiveness on the part of the relatively rich or the relatively cultivated. There are, of course, no social clubs, and indeed (except as the Protestant cult may be regarded as such) there are no persisting voluntary associations in the village. There are temporary associations for immediate purposes. Any one man may join in the celebration of a novena; any one may enter into the performance of the festival in celebration of the patron saint; any man may join in the performance of a pagan rain ceremony. And—with exceptions brought about either by Protestantism or by individual lack of faith—anybody does. When a *jarana* is held, it is expected that anyone will come who wants to, and I have no reason to suppose that anyone feels excluded because it is not "his crowd." At such a dance a young man dances with the partner who attracts him or with the partner who is put opposite him. There is nothing in what we were able to learn about marriages and the making of marriages in recent years that suggests a class organization. That such a girl might be an unsuitable match with a certain boy because she is no virgin, or because she is not a hard worker, I have heard said. Young men were recently refused as suitors by a girl or her parents because the suitor was known to drink or because he was thought not to be industrious. We heard nothing to suggest unsuitability of a match because the social status of the one family was not that of the other. Protestantism makes for difficulty in arranging marriages—that is another matter. But I cannot find any indication that wealthier families are tending to confine the marriages of their daughters or their sons to spouses from other wealthier families. Several of the marriages of recent years took place between a daughter or a son of one of the three or four most influential and wealthy families and a son or daughter of a family newly come to Chan Kom or of a family with little property, and most of these marriages were admired and were fully solemnized.

Table 1 (which omits the solitary Mexican) compares the organization of the population into familial households in 1931 with that prevailing in 1948. In the "single-family households" one roof shelters a married couple (or a single person) with or without near-relatives all of whom carry on a single domestic economy. In the "multiple-family households" there are two domestic economies in a single house: two pairs of spouses, each with its own milpa, washing of clothes, and, in many of these cases, separate preparation of meals. Each of the "extended domestic families" of 1931 was composed of a married couple, their married sons and their daughters-in-law, all carrying on agriculture and most of the domestic tasks as a single enterprise. In 1948 these compound families have broken up: each of the sons has his own milpa and own arrangements for meals; and many of the sons have built their own houses. The inclusion of one "new" domestic family in the table (for 1948) is dubious. A family that in 1931 consisted of husband and wife and a number of unmarried children now lives in the

TABLE 1

COMPOSITION OF HOUSEHOLDS

	1931	1948
Single-family households:		
Couple, with or without children..............	24	48
Couple living with man's unmarried parent or with other older relative...................	4	3
Couple and secondary wife...................	2	3
Widow, with unmarried children.............	3	4
Widow living alone........................	0	2
Brother and sisters........................	0	1
Unmarried man living alone.................	0	1
Total.................................	33	62
Multiple-family households:		
Two married brothers living together..........	3	0
Married brother and married sister...........	1	4
Couple living with man's parents.............	4	7
Couple living with wife's parents.............	1	2
Couple living with his paternal uncle and wife..	1	0
Two married friends living together...........	0	1
Total.................................	10	10
Extended domestic families:		
Married sons living in single economy with their parents..............................	2	1
Total number of households..............	45	73

same house where they lived before; several of the sons are married; these sons and their wives share the furniture and the kitchen of the house with the parental couple, and all eat together at a meal prepared by all the women. But each of the sons has his own small milpa, and each of the women her own hens. The father directs commercial operations in which the sons participate; I do not know how the gains are distributed.

The table shows how similar is the familial organization of 1948 to that of 1931. The single-family households preponderate as they did before. As before, the family consisting of parents and children is by far the commonest arrangement. In those households where a child continues to live with his parents after marriage, the double home is that of the young husband's parents, rather than that of the young wife's, in about the same proportion of cases; this reflects the prevailing and traditional emphasis on the father-son connection. There are three households (where before there were two) in which one man lives with two women. This kind of domestic arrangement lies outside of formal recognition: there is no ritual, no term, and no accepted role for the secondary woman. Nor does the arrangement reflect any trend, or any tradition, that I can discover. In all three cases the man involved is highly respected, and in two of them he is a leading citizen. In two, if not in all three, the secondary woman is respected as among women for one or another special skill and for good character. The arrangement is not condemned in comment or in gesture; the cases are spoken of with mild interest, no more.

It is perhaps notable that in so small a community, where marriage is so taken for granted as the natural condition of adults, six widows live without remarriage and direct their own households. But three widows so lived in 1931, and I was told that "it has always been so." A woman can live alone, on capital, her own labor, the help of her kinsmen, or charity (these widows, varyingly, depend on all four), more easily than can a man, whose domestic inconvenience is great if he has no one to cook and to work for him. Two of the widows living unremarried in Chan Kom today are still young and have refused excellent offers of marriage, preferring to live with their young children.

The reduced proportion of multiple-family households (22–14 per cent) is probably to be attributed to the increase in wealth, especially as expended in the construction of houses; those who wish to live separate from kinsmen have the means to do so. Yet on the average more people (6.0 as compared with 5.6) live in one house than did so in 1931. This increase must reflect chiefly an increase in the percentage of children surviving, an increase since 1940, when the proportion of children to the total population was the same as in 1931. The disappearance, or near-disappearance, of the patrilinear extended domestic family, already mentioned, probably does represent a real trend of change. In other respects, that will be noted, young people are less dependent upon the old than they were, and it is not likely that families will again form in which an older man directs the agricultural labors of his married sons into the profits of a single treasury, for him to manage, and in which his wife directs the domestic labors of her daughters-in-law. In earlier days some of these large households included the orphaned children of a man's brother or even of a man's sister. The obligation to bring up orphaned nephews persists, but young people more readily leave the home on marrying or on reaching maturity.

In ceasing to be single households, these two or three patriarchal extended families have by no means lost their solidarity. The solidarity of the patrilineal great families is no less in 1948 than it was in 1931. These are the social groups, larger than the component parental families, that were and that still are important in Chan Kom. It is common to hear such phrases as: "We are all —— [giving the paternal surname]." "It does not matter if you take that work to him or to me; we are both X's." "No, he does not come out much [to talk and mix with other people]. All the

Y's are like that." It is assumed that one will go first for
help to one's father, one's brother, one's paternal uncle, or
to one of those first cousins (called "brothers") that bear
one's own surname. Within these familial groups there is
much visiting, borrowing, and sharing of work. A woman
tends to assume the loyalty of her husband; at least it may
be said that her relatives have secondary claims; if there is
a conflict between her patrilineal family and his, the interests of his family prevail. On the other hand, the fact of her
connection with the rival family softens the conflict and is
a basis for resolving it. "After all, we are brothers-in-law."

Of course not everyone in Chan Kom is a member of a
large, well-established great family. There are recent emigrants who came to Chan Kom as single small families, and
there are the remnants of great families whose other members have moved away. Most of the inhabitants, however,
have in the village (and in almost every case living near
them) one or more families headed by a brother, father,
uncle, or cousin. In twenty-six households the head of the
family is a Tamay, a Pat, a Ceme, an Ek, or a Dzul. Four
of these groups are particularly cohesive and prominent in
village affairs.

These great families are no less significant than they
were in 1931 and are more conspicuous than they were
then. Now that many people live in houses set close to one
another along streets, the grouping of houses occupied by
patrilineal relatives is very marked. One side of the plaza is
"where the Pats live"; the Tamays occupy an adjacent
corner; the Cemes occupy half of a second side and a part
of a third side. Each of these groups has its own oven and
store and a well from which to draw water—or the near-by
cenote. The women in each group do their washing and
other work in walled yards each of which is a sort of family
compound—the Ceme family, more spread out than the
others, includes several such. The clusters of men who sit
together in the plaza outside the houses in the evening are

clusters of Pats, Tamays, or Cemes, with occasional additions from other families or from one of the other clusters. The Ek family, newcomers, form the nucleus of the "colony" or "suburb" west of the plaza and constitute a fourth conspicuous neighborhood group.

The emphasis upon interfamily competition brought about by the development of commerce and practical arts has been remarked in an earlier chapter. The store owned by a man of one of these families is not thought of as a rival of another store operated by other members of the same family, but the latter store in its competition with the store of another family has given rise to considerable bitterness. The two mills attract different customers; those who patronize the one mill belong to or have reason to commit themselves to the family operating it. The learning to play musical instruments has resulted in the formation not of one band but of two; and the competition between the Ceme band and the Tamay band is notorious—especially when they practice simultaneously, each in one of the only two second-floor rooms in the village.

Except at the time of the struggle over religion that will be reported in later pages, no decisive sentiments have prevented the people of Chan Kom from continuing to use throughout all these years the traditional institution of compulsory collective labor for the common good. This institution, *fagina*, has two forms: the obligation of all men not in public office to take their turns as guards or police officers and the obligation of all male citizens to contribute labor and materials on special occasions to public works. The first kind of *fagina* is continuous. It operates today when the community is the headquarters of a *municipio* very much as it did even before the village was a pueblo; there are more guards, and their responsibilities are greater, that is all. The other form of *fagina* has not been employed in recent years with the frequency with which it was employed during the strenuous years from 1928 to 1935, when the people were striving to build the streets, walls, and public buildings appropriate to a pueblo. It has been used, however, upon less frequent occasions since 1935. The men of the village were twice called upon in 1947 to perform labor on public improvements: once to dig a well in connection with the school and once to cement the floor of the "municipal palace."

It is not in the family, not in the organization of the people of Chan Kom as they carry on their own immediate affairs, that a new formality or a new impersonality is to be recognized, but in the institutions that have come into being as a result of the fact that Chan Kom has become first a pueblo and then the seat of the entire regional municipality. There are more offices to be filled than there were. As before, Chan Kom has its Socialist League, its Agrarian Committee, and its School Committee. The first two of these organizations relate the political affairs of the community to state-wide organizations but relate them in a manner hardly more than perfunctory: the duties of the officers of these bodies in Chan Kom are light and consist chiefly of receiving and answering official correspondence. The School Committee is called upon for some action or responsibility when the school inspector comes periodically to the village to see if the children are attending school as required and to look into the progress in education achieved under the teachers. These are old groups and offices. Here it may be added that, since the construction of a masonry church, the village has brought about an organization to manage the affairs of the church: two managers (*priostes*), two chanters (*maestros cantores*), four sacristans, and their three younger assistants (*mayoles*). This organization reflects the traditions as to church organization with which the people are familiar. It is, of course, an organization for affairs internal to the village only.

The important new offices are those of the new municipality: the municipal president (in place of the *comi-sario*, the chief political officer of a pueblo), his secretary, his assistants, and their substitutes—six in all; the justice of the peace; the registrar; the postmaster. Consistent with the increased population and enlarged responsibilities, the police force, consisting at one time or another of practically all the young men of the village, has been more than doubled. The principal offices are filled by the few Spanish-speaking men with recognized qualities of leadership; occasionally an officer succeeds himself, and one who has held a principal office may again assume that office after a lapse of years. At any one time most of the adult men are holders of one office or another.

The functions of these new political officers extend outside of Chan Kom itself, over the people of a dozen scattered settlements. The registrar records the births, deaths, and marriages of people whom he hardly knows, and in a certain discretion which he exercises in deciding whether a marriage shall be recorded or how the parentage of a child shall be entered, he affects the private lives of people of other settlements as well as those of his own. The justice of the peace and the municipal president have authority to conduct hearings and take evidence with regard to all sorts of civil and criminal complaints and to decide and punish delinquencies of all but the gravest sort. In the exercise of these powers they confront many an outsider to the village. So there is an impersonality and a formality of political and juridical relations which did not exist before in Chan Kom. The *comisario* of 1931 went about persuading, adjuring, and exhorting; he looked into disputes within families and strove to compose them by counsel and warning, if afterward by punishment. Today one does not see any local officer so functioning, like an elected father of the community. A citizen's difficulties in getting along with two women in his household, a man's complaint against his wife for adultery—these were matters that concerned the old *comisario* and concerned him as an informal leader. Today there comes to the municipal president such matters as the law of the state and the nation declare should come before him. The judge is literate and consults a printed summary of the laws. The judge and the municipal president operate more closely under review of the authorities of Merida or Dzitas. These differences, so plainly seen by one who comes back to the village after fifteen years, are in part reflections of differences in the personalities of the *comisario* of the earlier day and the municipal president of the present day; but I have seen that former *comisario* function on formal occasions in 1948, and he has changed his ways: the formal law is much better known now, and the proceedings are more impersonal.

In short, such change as has taken place in the social relations of the people of Chan Kom is chiefly a change in the relations they have with outsiders. This change is incident to the rise of the village to political and economic preeminence within its little region. The Chan Kom people exercise new authority in a wider community. They are becoming used to people who come to them to get justice done, as they become used to people who come to them to sell venison or tomatoes or to buy in the Chan Kom stores. The villagers have the confidence of successful men. They look, from something of an eminence, toward "backward" *rancherías* within their *municipio*. And correspondingly they have become more familiar with city people and their ways and feel themselves more at ease than they used to be when townsmen of business or of government come among them.

But in the relations the Chan Kom people have with one another, there has been no great change. The population has almost doubled, and the political authority has been achieved, without making Chan Kom over. It is still a community of one kind of people: rural, Maya toilers in the milpa; these people have added cattle-raising, business, and government to their activities. The new population shares with the old a common tradition, emphasizing industry and an earthy piety. All these people, old and new, think of themselves as Indians and as a people belonging to the bush, the milpa, and the settlement around the cenote. The increased experience with law and government has added a formality and a certain impersonality to proceedings that obey these sources of authority, but I cannot see that the personal and familial nature of the paramount social controls has been as yet significantly changed. The increase in size of the community and the rise to power have not changed the simple social structure of small family households grouped into patrilineal great families. It is still these family connections that principally guide conduct. And the same great families, on the whole, that prevailed seventeen years ago, today provide the leadership. When a decision is to be made, as formerly, the principal men of a family talk together, and then leaders of different families talk together, so that agreement on most issues is reached before any public action is taken. No new association, no new form of grouping, has been found necessary to carry on the enlarged affairs of the community.

Nevertheless, the foregoing statement ignores the one important new association that has appeared in Chan Kom in these years: the Protestant church. The sense of solidarity of the members of the village as a whole is not quite so great as it was in 1931, and the antagonisms between certain of the great families are more apparent. Of this change the new religion is the chief cause. The unity of the community and the always delicate balance of power and peace among the great families received from the advent of the evangelical missionaries a shock which almost frustrated the strong impulse of the people toward progress and material success.

V

The Great Schism

I F THE words "religion" and "Catholic" were used in 1930 by the people of Chan Kom, I cannot recall the fact. Neither conception was sufficiently emphasized to bring about inclusion of the corresponding word in the index of the book that describes the life of the community at that time. The idea of religion, as a body of faith and practice pursued by one member of the community but not by others, was, I am sure, then absent from the thinking of the villagers. At least people did not talk about their "religion." Men talked about the acts they had performed or would perform: one said one would today "take corn meal out to the milpa" or that one had last night "burned three candles to San Diego." The ceremonies of appeal to unseen powers or in propitiation of them were an inseparable part of the daily conduct of life.

The idea of a Catholic religion as distinct from some other kind did not appear. The same ceremonial forms were employed by all the villagers. All of them expressed in the same way their piety and their wish for virtuous and prudent relationships with unseen powers. The origins of the rituals were, to the villagers, lost in antiquity or recognized in mythology that had been told them by their grandfathers who had learned it from their grandfathers. That in fact part of their beliefs and rituals came to them from Indian sources and another part from Spanish sources was not recognized. The people knew a single traditional authority, a single piety. They did indeed recognize two kinds of rituals, but these two they identified not with differences

88

in historical origins or with authorities or principles in conflict with one another but with the forms appropriate to
each and especially with the functionaries who led them.
There were the ceremonies conducted by the chanter
(*maestro cantor*) before the images of the saints; and there
were the ceremonies led by that other functionary, the
h-men, who built his altar not within any building but under the sky in the milpa or in the wood and who included in
his appeals (in his case expressed in the Maya language and
not in Spanish or Latin) certain beings who were thought
to dwell in the forest, the cenote, or the sky. These were
two kinds of rituals, both available to all the people, and
both used, successively, in situations of serious crisis. The
ceremonies of the *h-men* were not opposed in faith or merit
to those led by the chanter. Both rested under the Great
God; the Virgin, the Holy Cross, and certain of the saints
were celebrated in both; both were parts of a common faith
and morality. It occurred to no one to choose between
these or to choose some way of utterance of faith different
from this one double way, and doubt as to its truth or
worth did not appear.

Nevertheless, some of the people of the village were by
the year 1930 aware of the appearance in other communities of their territory, and notably in the village of Piste,
near Chichen Itza, of the bearers of a new cult. There was
probably even at that time discussion of these "evangelists"
of which I was not aware. A document prepared in later
years by the Protestant missionaries names a teacher who
taught in Chan Kom before 1927—before Villa came there
—as the first Protestant in that village. In talking to us of
the history of the new cult, the people have not mentioned
this man. The event that was important in this connection
occurred in 1931. The new school building had collapsed
not long before, shocking the people with the tragedy of the
sudden death of the villager killed in the ruins, giving rise

to speculations as to portents and punishments, and cooling the enthusiasm for progress and public works. The leaders of the community found themselves unable to summon the efforts of the people to rebuild the school, and the catastrophe had made people doubt their leadership. At this state of affairs there appeared in the village a pair of hog-drovers from Dzitas who spoke to the people of Chan Kom "of the true teaching of the Lord," and showed them Bibles, telling them that anyone who followed the advice laid down in that book might be assured of God's support.

Moreover, they made that connection between Protestantism and progress which was so important a factor in bringing about its acceptance in Chan Kom. They told the villagers that the people of the towns and the city were Protestants and that the Americans—a people then coming into importance among the villagers as powerful and admirable—were Protestants too. At the same time they emphasized humility, gentleness, and self-sacrifice. They told of the sufferings and abnegation of the martyrs. The leaders of Chan Kom (with whom in this connection the teacher Villa joined) saw in this last theme the way to restore the flagging determination of the people. Partly by the deliberate action of these leaders, self-denial and the example of the martyrs became a central theme of conversation and a model held up before the people. The people agreed to begin again on the building of the school. The influence of the leaders was re-established. Don Eus and the others saw in the missionaries new and valuable allies.

The leaders of the village accepted the suggestion of the hog-driving evangelists that there be sent to the village a teacher better prepared than were these forerunners. When this man came—probably a missionary employed by the evangelical mission established by North Americans in the state of Yucatan—he was welcomed by the leaders of the principal families and provided with food and shelter and with a house in which to conduct his teaching. The people gathered before a table spread with an embroidered cloth on which stood bunches of flowers—as in their own traditional domestic rituals—and the new holy object: a Bible. The preaching was in Maya. It was repeated on successive nights; the meetings were well attended; several of the villagers bought New Testaments of the missionary.

During 1931 and part of 1932 the evangelizing effort was energetic and frequently repeated. The missionaries strove to convert to the new faith this rising village, deep in the bush but obviously a progressive community prepared to lead the people of its region. Two missionaries made extended visits. A portable organ was brought, and hymns were taught. Later, for periods of more than a week, groups of six or eight town-educated Protestants, including several women, stayed in Chan Kom to preach and to conduct prayer meetings. A local congregation was formally organized in 1932, with a board of directors consisting of three men of Chan Kom.

By the summer of 1932 the community was apparently converted to Protestantism. Except for half-a-dozen families, all the people of Chan Kom were attending Protestant services. These had now been transferred to the civic building ("Municipal Palace") so that all the people might be present. Thus an official approval, by the local government, was given to the new movement. The *comisario*, the head of this government, was at this time Don Eus Ceme. This man, the most energetic and influential of the village leaders, labored to help the missionaries. He took into his charge arrangements for the meeting and for the comfort and convenience of the missionaries. The little thatched church was closed; no services took place there. The effigy of San Diego, the village patron, was removed to the house of the Tamay family, one of the few that would have nothing to do with the new religion; and the day of the saint came and went without any public celebration. Most of the people of Chan Kom were talking of the new cult, attending its meetings, and studying its tenets through the words of the missionaries and discussion among themselves. It was said in neighboring settlements that Chan Kom had turned *Evangelista*.

Only in appearance, however, was this transformation a further expression of the unity and social solidarity of the village. The conversion itself, in so far as it was real and permanent, rested upon a factional division that had long existed within the community and was soon to accentuate that division.

Since the very founding of the village, the population of Chan Kom has always contained two principal family groups: the Ceme family and the Pat family. On each of these lesser families have been dependent. At the time of the coming of the evangelists the Tamays and the Ucs were connected with the Cemes, the Caamals and the Kuyocs with the Pats. Intermarried though they were, the two factions were in competition and rivalry. The rivalry was for prestige as expressed in wealth, education, and religious leadership and for political control of the community. Yet the necessity to maintain solidarity as against the competition of other villages in the rise to power was felt by the community, and the leadership of the village was good enough to keep the rivalry within the village from being disruptive. If a desirable house site was provided to a family of one faction, a corresponding house site was provided to the other. As the slates of officers for the local government were made up, representatives of both factions were included, or it was seen to that if Cemes had had the leading post for two or three years, the Pat group should be recognized in the next year. In the organization of *novenarios* and rain ceremonies, both factions were invariably included among the principals. In the early years the competition was usually friendly; if there was rancor, it did not burst forth.

But in power and success the two factions were unequal. The Cemes on the whole prevailed over the Pats. They acquired wealth more rapidly than did the Pats. They provided more effective leaders than did the Pats. The Cemes had more men who spoke Spanish and were literate than did the rival family, and this fact alone gave to the Cemes an advantage. Moreover, the Tamays, who were associated with the Cemes, had for family head the village *maestro cantor* and marriage negotiator—a sort of lay priest in the community. And the effigy of San Diego, the patron, was owned by the Tamays.

It must have been this last fact which led the Pats, before Protestantism was heard of in Chan Kom, to buy a blessed effigy of the Infant Jesus and to instal it in the house of one of the three married brothers of this name. The Pats instituted a cult of the *Niño Dios* which was an expression of the solidarity of their own family group as against the Cemes, and did so, as had to be the case at that time, within the cultural and religious conceptions that were common to the entire village. The foundation of the coming schism was laid in the attention which the Pats now gave to the cult of the Child God, and the corresponding slackening of attention which they gave to the cult of San Diego—the patron, but a patron especially associated with the Cemes and the Tamays. At this time disease struck suddenly at hogs and poultry, and when the Tamays proposed that a novena be held in the hope of ridding the village of these plagues, the Pats objected and urged instead that the affected animals be removed from the village to distant milpas. The will of the former group was realized, and when the novena was held, and rain fell as a sign of grace, the prestige of the Cemes and Tamays, through the saint associated with them, was increased. The readiness of the winning faction to recognize the danger to unity from such an occurrence, and their willingness to do something to restore the unity, were exemplified in this instance, for soon thereafter novenas were held in honor of the Infant Jesus and then in honor of the Holy Cross—a symbol common to all in the village and all the Maya of that territory.

These events, which took place before 1930, help us to understand why it was that the Pats were in the forefront of those who adopted Protestantism in 1931–32. In 1931 the *comisario* was a Ceme, and a Ceme of great energy and determination. His leadership was almost a rule, and under its exacting demand of frequent compulsory labor on public works and its policy of stern punishment for infractions of this rule, the Pats felt their disadvantage as the suffering of a tyranny. For years they had taken the short end of the stick, and now they found themselves compelled to toil and to obey the great rival family. The appearance of the new religion gave them an opportunity to gain prestige in a new circle, a new set of associates, and to feel a fresh sense of their own righteousness. To impute these interests and motives to the Pats is not to deny that the new religion gave them, or some of them, more fundamental and more admirable satisfactions. Their conversion led them to greater self-control, and in the new faith they conquered their previous tendencies to quarrelsomeness and intemperance.

By opening their homes to the missionaries, the Pats associated themselves with these valued representatives of the progressive and better way of life. By putting forward their literate and Spanish-speaking sons as readers of the new sacred texts, the older men of this family in a way overcame the disadvantages of their own illiteracy and ignorance of Spanish. Young people could not be used to take leading places in the traditional religion, for those roles are of course appropriate to the old, but in the new religion youth was no disadvantage. One young Pat in particular became the first assistant of the missionaries; he devoted himself to study of the Bible and of the explanatory materials provided him; he read passages aloud at the gatherings of the cult and developed a new *persona*—that of an austere, self-disciplining zealot, withdrawn from light affairs and earthly pleasures. The Pats became very proud of this young man. But to an older Ceme, the conduct of this young person looked very different, especially when persons older than he came to consult with him on spiritual matters.

This first phase of the period of conversion to Protestantism may be recognized in a general movement of the community toward adoption of the new religion. The community, striving in general to adopt ways of life associated with the city and progress, was at once favorably disposed toward the new teaching, coming as it did with just these associations. Furthermore, the old traditional virtues of industry and sobriety (sobriety in the workaday world) had been especially emphasized in Chan Kom: as compared with other communities in the territory, this village had a reputation for abstinence from drink and for hard work, both in private endeavor and in public constructions. To labor, produce, and limit one's pleasures so as not to waste resources of strength and wealth—these had been for years the teachings of the village leaders. The new missionaries taught sobriety, too, and self-denial. We may also suppose that the anticlerical policies of the Mexican government, and the strong attack upon the Catholic hierarchy made in public discussion in the cities at just this time, exerted its influence, although remotely, upon Chan Kom. Then, too, no priest had ever lived in Chan Kom. It was a long journey on foot to Valladolid when a newborn baby had to be carried through the bush to the priest for baptism. The Protestants offered a ritual of baptism and made it available right there in the village.

The missionaries of the new way of life required much more, however, than to stay sober and to work hard. They required that men give up a very great deal of what made life interesting. They not only told them that baptism by a priest and marriage by a priest were wrong, but they also told the people that it was wrong to appeal to the saints and even to maintain in their houses and in their church the effigies—the *santos* in whose care the people of the village had remained safe for so many years, and to whom they had appealed, year after year when their crops were threatened or their children were sick. Candles, too, those blooms of prayerful offering on the dark altars, were pronounced sinful, and all the chants that they had learned to hear or to make at times of need and hope. And, striking still more acutely into the joy of life, the missionaries forbade their converts to dance. The dance, the *jarana*, was the ancient form of rhythmic art and the chief opportunity of self-expression and social delight. The *jaranas*, held at every important festival, to glorify a saint or to honor a visitor, provided the only occasions on which the women could leave the confinement and obscurity of their domestic lives, the only occasions when they could shine forth, the only evenings when they could wear their beloved *ternos*—the fine dresses on which they spent so many hours of labor and creative effort, with the gold chains and earrings of which they and their husbands were so proud. All this, the new teachers said, in effect, would be used no more.

From the many accounts provided of these years, it is plain that from the first the rigor and scope of these requirements brought dismay to many. Almost from the first some of those who accepted *Evangelismo* drew back from accepting its injunctions in full. The Ceme who was at the time *comisario* stressed that part of the new teaching which emphasized obedience and discipline. And he expressed the opinion, at first in small groups but in no public assembly, that dancing in particular was not wrong. Having in mind the modern dances which some of the villagers were now beginning to learn (from visitors to the village more secular than the Protestant missionaries), and which were now sometimes danced in the evening to music of a phonograph, the *comisario* pointed out that the Americans danced them and that all information showed that they were a favorite source of delight to civilized people generally. With this view the Tamays, in whose house these dances took place, agreed.

The Pats, however, disagreed. The Pats accepted the new teaching in full and even added to it a few austerities; they were heard to argue that it was wrong to take a little excursion, for mere pleasure, to another village. The second phase of the movement toward conversion appears in the assumption of its leadership by the Pats and in the consequent recognition of two groups of converts: the moderates and the extremists. The Pats busied themselves in providing the tablecloths and flowers for the missionaries and pressed their hospitality upon them. The Pats became zealots in their search for purity of soul. They gave up not only the smoking of tobacco but even its cultivation—a recent horticultural revival in Chan Kom. The Pats put their *santo* quite away; they used candles no more in any ritual, and they let it be known that they would not again attend a *jarana*. There came a time when the missionaries had to take account of these two groups of converts; frankly in opposition to each other now, each faction pressed the teachers for a statement as to where the right position lay. The missionaries upheld the extremists. In a sermon one of them explicitly supported the Pats, naming them as exemplary brothers in the faith. Indeed, in this

same sermon the missionary declared that the "cultural reunions" so dear to the heart of the *comisario*, in which educational or uplifting subjects were discussed, must be abandoned as frivolous and outside the true religion. It was immediately after this sermon that the directoral board of the
new congregation was chosen. The missionaries guided the
selection; chosen as chairman was the young Pat described
above, and no Ceme was included. The missionary rubbed
it in: he advised the brethren to consult with this young
Pat concerning any doubts they might hold as to the new
faith. At this meeting little attention was paid to the
Cemes or the Tamays. The lines were now drawn, but still
drawn within the congregation of the new converts—
almost all the community.

At this same time, under the leadership of the *comisario*,
the village was striving to attain recognition from the national government of status as an independent municipality. It was opposed by the rival and already established
municipality of Cuncunul. Chan Kom was trying to bring
within its sphere of influence hamlets of the region whose
inhabitants inclined now to Chan Kom and now to Cuncunul. A division within Chan Kom threatened the success
of the movement to defeat Cuncunul and to make Chan
Kom a "free municipality" with a strong group of satellite
settlements. The *comisario* of Chan Kom (a Ceme) sought
to preserve the unity of his village. Even after the meeting
just referred to he made an effort for compromise. Taking
with him another village leader, a man not a Ceme and yet
unconnected with the Pats, he visited the missionary then
resident in Chan Kom and, speaking in his official capac-
ity, urged the missionary to stop talking against cultural
reunions and against the patron saint. He proposed that
the missionary confine his activities to teaching hymns and
explaining stories from the Bible. The missionary did not
refuse the suggestions, but he did not act on them, and

when that night a dance was held in the Tamay house, he and his associates stayed away. The division in the community had gone too far to stop.

Now the Cemes were becoming sure that they could not accept the uncompromising Protestantism of the Pats. They could not, and their women especially would not, give up all that becoming a Protestant required. And to submit to leadership from the rival faction, especially when embodied in untried youth or distrusted outsider, was not to be endured. And, further, pressure upon the community to remain in the old-time religion was increasing from the inhabitants of the bush villages in the neighborhood. These more isolated people were turning away from the leadership of Chan Kom. They came less and less to the store in Chan Kom; when a group of them butchered a hog, they no longer brought the meat to Chan Kom; and some of them, meeting Chan Kom people on the trails, mocked at them as wicked, as people turning their backs on the saints that protected them.

When once Don Eus, the *comisario*, was convinced that he could not go forward and that no compromise was possible, he turned back. Having led his people into the new religion, he proceeded to lead most of them out of it. The turn came toward the end of the second year after the village had been apparently converted to Protestantism. An indication of the new policy appeared in the announcement by the *comisario* that the Mexican law forbade the use of public buildings for religious services and that therefore the Protestants could no longer use the "Municipal Palace" for their meetings.

The open break came on the occasion of the celebration of the Day of the Holy Cross (the third of May). It will be recalled that the Tamays were among those few who at no time accepted any part of the new cult and who maintained in their house the effigy of the patron saint. The Tamays now announced that they would celebrate the Day of the Cross—symbol of all Mayas and thus an auspice of unity—with a *jarana* in their house and that good musicians had been arranged for. There was at once talk about how sad this *jarana* would be, with only the Tamays present. The missionaries announced a prayer meeting for the night on which the *jarana* was to be held. The *comisario* moved back and forth, consulting with the principal men of his faction, consulting with the missionaries. It is probable that he made known to the leading men of his group what he was about to do.

The Cemes attended the prayer meeting as did of course the Pats. Only the Tamays were not there. The meeting lasted until late, and, as it concluded, the music for the *jarana*, the heart-stirring music for the *jarana*, began in the Tamay house. The missionaries spoke of the evils of dancing, announced that a prayer meeting would be held at six the next morning, and impressed upon their hearers the importance of attendance. The *comisario* said nothing at the meeting, but at its close he brought together the principal men and told them that as he was a public official, and the law forbade the use of public buildings for religious uses, he felt he had no choice but to withdraw from the new religion. He added that he was about to take his wife and two daughters to the Tamay *jarana*.

It was then about midnight. The missionaries had put away their melodeon. The *jarana* music was very loud in the Tamay house. From many another house eyes looked out, watching the house on the plaza where lived the *comisario*. At last, at about one in the morning, the four figures emerged and, walking a few steps down the plaza, entered the house of the Tamays. Within half an hour, dozens of other dancers, clad in their best, had arrived there too, and the *jarana*, one of the liveliest in Chan Kom history, lasted until dawn.

But the Cemes went to the six o'clock prayer meeting. There was still something that they had to do. They heard the sermon that heaped condemnation upon them to its end. The *comisario* then arose and said in substance: We have come to say goodbye. We say it in a friendly spirit. But we cannot follow you. Your laws are not for us. We are far away, here in the bush. We must divert ourselves, once in a while, by dancing. And look, there in the plaza the new outdoor theater has been built; we have been told by our schoolteachers that it is to be used as a place to hear songs and music and cultural programs. We cannot give up all that. And you teach us that riches too are bad, and that if a man has ten cows he must give one to the evangelical association. But we want to have wealth. So you had better not stay with us. Our Chan Kom has been well planned. We have always been united, united with the civilized pueblos that enjoy their fiestas and increase their wealth.

From this time forward there were two religious communities in Chan Kom. The majority of the people resumed the cult of the saints with a devotion greater than prevailed before. These people assembled again in the houses to participate in the novenas led by the chanter, the effigy of San Diego was returned to the little church, and the festival of the patron was again celebrated. Dancing, of both traditional and modern kinds, was resumed. Now it was an evident majority who did these things, and the Protestants were no longer assumed to stand together with this majority in public affairs. After this no Pat and no Protestant became *comisario* or municipal president. The majority withdrew from the Protestants almost as the Protestants withdrew from the majority. In the first years after the division, the followers of the traditional religion did not attend prayer meetings of the Protestants. The Ceme leader told his people that it was not seemly for civilized people to be present at meetings of the cult. His principal object was achieved; most of the community went forward now under his guidance, and the people of the neighboring settlements, reassured by the turn of events, once more joined in the effort to make Chan Kom an independent municipality. In 1935 this was accomplished.

The Protestants now conducted their prayer meetings in the house of one of the Pats. Shut away in their group of adjoining houses, they carried forward in seclusion the cult of their faith. They were now a religious minority and, in their own view, a persecuted minority. What they learned from their religious teachers of the lives of the early martyrs helped them to define and to bear their new role. They were bitter, but they were also long-suffering.

Not all the Cemes returned to the traditional religion at the time that the *comisario* announced his withdrawal from Protestantism. Two of the younger married men of that family remained for a year or two within the Protestant congregation. These were the two young men of the village most experienced in town ways and far advanced in the assumption of the clothing and the manners of the newer way of life. With the Pats remained also several other lesser families who had connection by marriage with the Pats, or who at least had no close connection with the Cemes. In 1935 Steggerda reported eight Protestant families in Chan Kom. The census of 1940 listed thirty-four persons as Protestants, and twenty-five as "of no religion." (Children under five were assigned the religion of their parents.) By 1948 the Protestants of Chan Kom consisted of one large extended domestic family of Pats and one or possibly two small families of other surnames.

In the years between 1935 and 1948 a partial restoration of unity was achieved, on the one hand, by elimination from the community of families that adhered to Protes-

tantism and, on the other, by the development of accom-
modation between the two religious groups.

Once out in the open, the conflict between Protestants
and those who had now learned to call themselves "Catholics" was attended with bitterness and occasional violence.
At once dissension became marked in connection with the
construction of a masonry Catholic church. This was an
old project: for many years the village leaders had talked
of it and had told themselves that, when the other buildings, more immediately necessary, had been built, a new
church would be erected. A thatched structure of poles was
not suitable as a church for a people who had made their
community a pueblo. By custom, all such public works are
constructed by the unpaid labor of the inhabitants who, as
an aspect of their obligations as citizens, are compelled,
under penalty of jail sentence, to share in the work. But
when the first assignments to prepare beams and to burn
lime for the new church were announced, the Protestants
declared that they would not "build for the *santos*." A
compromise, proposed by the ingenious Don Eus Ceme, always seeking to harmonize the conflicting groups, that a
curtain be hung in the new church after the altar was built
so that the Pats would not work in the presence of the
saints, was refused, and in the course of resulting argument
two elders, one of each faction, came to blows. Don Eus,
then municipal president, jailed the Protestant combat-
ants. Released, one or more of them went to Merida to
lodge a complaint against the village administration (the
Cemes) as tyrannical and unjust. A group in the state or
national government, anti-Catholic in sympathy, supported them, but another group in the city sent word to
Don Eus that he must be on guard against the Protestants,
for they were ungodly ones supported by a dangerous element in foreign lands known as "Communists." Accordingly, Don Eus at first redoubled his discipline of the local

Protestants. But later he removed the immediate cause of conflict: it was agreed that construction of the church would be postponed. The people, Protestants and Catholics alike, went to work on a new house for the schoolteachers. And the church issue was eventually solved, more or less, when the local authorities allowed the Protestants to work on a construction of a Protestant chapel, also to be a public building, instead of laboring on the Catholic church. But it was then that the Cemes who had remained Protestants at last broke away—unable, apparently, to withstand the pressure of their kinsmen who were working at the same time on another building on the opposite side of the plaza, they quarreled with the Pats and returned to the old-time religion.

In the meantime other disputes arose between the factions. Under some claim of authority the municipal president ordered cut down a large cedar that stood near the house of one of the Protestants. Urged by the Pats, the houseowner at first refused to obey the order and then cut the tree down and made himself some washing trays from the wood. He was jailed, and, when some of the Pats tried to prevent the arrest, they were jailed too. Then the president ordered an old and unoccupied house built by the Pats to be torn down so as to make room for erection of a house to provide for a new settler. The new settler was not a Protestant. The Pats tried to prevent the tearing-down of the old structure and then to prevent the building of a house for the new inhabitant; and again they were jailed. On this occasion they worked out a fine of one hundred loads of weathered limestone building material, excavated from the pits and carried on their backs to the village. Exasperated beyond endurance, having failed to enlist the aid of the outside government, two of the three principal Pat families withdrew from Chan Kom in 1938, to settle in hamlets not far away. And at this time, or a little later, other Protestant families left too.

In their new homes these *émigrés* continued the struggle. Certain of them who settled in X-Kopteil, a settlement belonging to the *municipio* of which Chan Kom was now the seat of the local government, now led a movement to separate X-Kopteil from the *municipio* of Chan Kom and attach it to the *municipio* of Yaxcaba. This was doubly treacherous, in the view of the Ceme faction, for Yaxcaba belonged in the western territory that was traditionally unfriendly to Chan Kom. The Pats were joined in this separatist effort by other Protestant families in other hamlets depending upon Chan Kom. The group thus formed tried either to detach certain settlements from Chan Kom and attach them to Yaxcaba or to establish a new independent municipality. They were of course opposed by the Catholic elements in their own settlements. The details of this struggle need not concern us here; violence followed and appeals to the national government, but the movement was unsuccessful.

Thus it was that, as the unity of the village of Chan Kom was once more approximated, the conflict between Protestant and Catholic was pushed outside of the village to become a fresh factor in the endless struggle for power between villages.

As this was going on, the people of Chan Kom, Protestant and Catholic, were learning to make adjustments to each others' ways so that a common life might be carried on. While the men of the village struggled with one another over the building of church and chapel, to the point of blows, in other sectors of life members of the two religious groups shared common interests and exchanged the human sympathies of neighbors and kinsmen.

Little by little the Protestants adopted again some of the practices which they gave up in the first zeal of conversion. In the store of the Pats candles, cigarettes, and perhaps rum became again available to purchasers. One of the Pats brought a bull to a festival of the patron saint of a neighboring settlement. Some of the Pats appeared at *jaranas*, not to dance, but to sit and watch. One of their young men, after a lapse of a few years, danced again in the *jaranas*, although still regarding himself as a Protestant. When All Souls' Day came around, the Pats set out food and flowers on a table with a new cloth, as was the traditional custom, and called upon their dead by name. Only the effigy of a saint and candles were missing from their little ritual. They performed the ritual appropriate to the day in a Protestant form. Apparently the missionaries had no part in this development; it was brought about by the converts out of their ancient belief that the souls of the dead return on that day and their sense of need to receive these souls in respect and in such a way as to get them safely back into the other world where they would not trouble the living. The effect was to unite the community once more, on that day, in a common recognition of an old custom, in a single expression of piety and prudence. And when death came, there was no division into separate congregations. One of the Pats, the mother of the converted brothers, died. Although she had apparently followed her sons into the new religion, and although Protestant prayers were recited, her daughter, married to a Ceme, saw to it that Catholic prayers were also read in the presence of all the relatives. And the Protestants established no burying ground of their own; this old lady was buried in the village cemetery where all who had preceded her there had been Catholics.

In periods when no important struggle between the two factions was going on, relationships between particular families became or were sufficiently friendly so that Catholics attended prayer meetings of the Protestants, and occasionally Protestants would participate, socially though not ritually, in a novena held in the house of a Catholic.

Moreover, in one quarter of the native tradition there remained undisturbed by the evangelical movement another basis for unity of the community. The people, Protestants and Catholics alike, continued to carry on, in common, the rituals presided over by the shaman priest and addressed not so much to the saints as to the Maya supernaturals of field, forest, and sky. It is reliably reported that in 1934, when the Cemes had withdrawn from the new religion and the struggle between the two factions was public and harsh, several of the Pats took part in the rain ceremony (*cha-chaac*) held in that year. In the same year certain of the principal Pats made the first-fruit ceremony (*pibil-nal*) requiring the services of the *h-men*, and in 1935 a man of this family called a *h-men* to attend his sick child and, on advice of the *h-men*, performed the *kex* ceremony whereby the infecting "evil winds" are bought off by the making of offerings and removed by lustrative rites. And from the accounts given in 1948 it appears that in subsequent years, and up to the time of recent observations, the Protestants continued to share in the rituals of pagan origin. They called the *h-mens* for sickness and carried out the therapeutic rituals he prescribed, and they took their places in the ceremony carried on by the entire group—the rain ceremony—that is addressed to the deities that ride the sky to bring the water necessary for the growth of maize and therefore for life itself.

The needs which are expressed in these ceremonies of pagan origin are the common and the deepest needs—for a good crop, for health, for preservation of life. It would have been even harder for men well enough content with affairs as they were to accept Protestantism if its missionaries had forbidden the practice of these pagan ceremonies. But apparently they did not forbid them. I cannot find that they said anything at all about them. In no account of their teachings that I have received from either convert or recanter is there mention of anything said by the missionaries about the cult that is conducted by the *h-men*. These missionaries apparently carried out the letter of the teaching they received from its distant American source: they spoke of the reading of the Bible, of matters of personal conduct, and of the error of praying to saints instead of directly to God. Their teaching had been cut to the cloth of a Catholicism different from that of the Maya village. So, behind the struggle to choose between the cult of the Bible and the Protestant prayer and the cult of the *santo* and the ancient ritual words there was continued common participation in the ceremonies of cornfield, beehive, and forest. The Protestants did, indeed, come in later years to carry on some of these ceremonies with less faithfulness than they had before, but so did some of the Catholics. There is nothing in the history of the Protestant movement in Chan Kom that suggests that it was its influence that brought about a decline, slight though it is to the present time, in the pagan cult.

In this connection it may be pointed out that the Protestant movement in Chan Kom presented to the villagers no important problems of faith or doctrine if by these words is meant a content of belief as to the nature of God, or the relation of man to God, or as to sin, salvation, or the problem of evil. Such topics are not mentioned in the discussions quoted to me as to religious differences in Chan Kom. I did not hear that either side threatened the other with hell's fire. The issues that the villager had to face were different. They were, as already indicated, in first place, issues as to the rightness and practical effectiveness of one kind of ritual as compared with another. And here, as just said, only one part of the ritual—that centering around the saint and the prayers of the chanter—was subject to attack. One gave up the worship in the church before the effigies of the saints in favor of worship before a Bible in a new chapel, or one did not. In the second place, there were questions as to the rightness of certain kinds of personal conduct: the Protestants enjoined a higher standard of abstinence and self-denial of pleasure than was usual according to the old tradition. The Protestant converts who remained converted did conspicuously change their personal manner of life. They drank less, fought less, and played and joked less than they had before. They felt themselves changed; they knew themselves more virtuous, humbler, more "decent" than they had been before. Those, who remained Catholics felt less need of making such a change, for they had less change to make.

These two kinds of issues—as to ritual practiced and as to rules of personal conduct—were of course presented to the villager uncertain as to the choice he should make, in particular situations of personal relationship and of leadership offered. To Villa, returning for a visit, the question was put: Who better explains the Bible, Don Eus (Ceme) or Tibo (the literate young man of the Pat family)? For Don Eus it was who first brought the Bible to Chan Kom and read from it to some of his neighbors, explaining the moral worth of the passages. The Bible was discovered by Don Eus without the aid of Protestantism. The question was, therefore: "Which leader shall I follow?" The two factional groups of families provided the poles around which leadership and power, in the struggle between Protestant and Catholic, became organized.

Within domestic families the new religion brought about no divisions. Wife and children followed the husband and father into the new religion, without exception, and in no Protestant household was there, even for a brief period, any notorious holdout for Catholicism. Nor did any one member of a Catholic family alone become a Protestant. All the Pat brothers of the older generation became Protestants, bringing all their several families with them. There was, however, one case in another lineage where one married brother became a Protestant while the other, also married, did not; and a wife of a Ceme, herself a Pat, remained a Catholic while all her married brothers and their families took up the new religion. This was to be expected in Chan Kom, where (as generally in Indian Middle America) a wife and her husband are one unit for ritual and public purposes. And the authority of parents over their children who are still in the household, though married, remains very great in Chan Kom.

These facts as to traditional family organization made it difficult for the young men of the converted families to find wives. The fathers who remained Catholics would not have Protestant son-in-laws. Not only would the problem of baptism of children arise, to divide the intermarried group, but the daughter would be lost to the ritual group and political faction of the father. In the case of the Pats, there were at home during these years one married son and three unmarried sons of marriageable age. The wife of the first became a Protestant with the rest of the family into which she had married. A second son married a Protestant girl from another village. A third married the daughter of a Chan Kom man who had just turned Protestant, but displeased the father-in-law, who later withdrew from Protestantism; the girl remained with her husband in the new religion. The fourth in 1948 attempted, against objection from the girl's parents, to arrange a marriage with a Catholic girl of the village. It is apparent that the difficulty of finding wives, after the schism developed, contributed to the decision of some of the Protestant families to move away to other settlements, in which there were more Protestants.

By 1948 the devisive effect upon the village of the Protestant movement had been largely overcome. At least it is true that by that time the people as a whole again moved forward on the paths of action set out for them by a leadership consistent within itself. The religion of this little society was again the religion of its forefathers, and all its leaders took part in it. Indeed, the return to Catholicism took place in a renewed zeal for traditional religious belief and practice. When the new church was completed, an organization of managers and custodians of the building and its cult was instituted, according to tradition; bells were hung upon the church, and matins and Angelus were vigorously, if somewhat irregularly, rung. On several evenings each week the chanter, or his new disciple, led a small group in prayers, and the more conspicuous position of the new church, with its wide-open doors, announced to all the comings and goings of the faithful to burn candles or to join in the litany. The church organization was closely interrelated with the local secular government, and once again all those who took part in the public life of the community joined in a single congregation.

The remaining Pat family, large though it was in numbers, was now a dissident island enclaved within the Catholic community. Its members remained much to themselves, provided with necessaries from the store kept in their house, with their own gristmill within the family compound, and the cenote right at hand from which to draw their water. Their associations with most of the others of the community are in all appearance friendly, but there is not very much association. Yet they have developed associations with some of the younger sons, now married, of their close neighbors, the Tamay family, and these Tamays join with the Pats in talk and work, use their mill, and buy in their store goods not available in their own. As the Tamays are by tradition associated with the Cemes, and as to some extent its members still claim that association, there is now no simple dual division within the village, and the Tamays, remaining Catholics, hold something of a balance of power, or, at least, limit the growing power of the Cemes. On the other hand, the Pats have many connections, personal and commercial, with other communities in which there are Protestants. Two of the sons operate family-owned gristmills in other villages. A Protestant society that transcends any local community, with loyalties to its own cult and membership rather than to each village, is developing.

The other one or two families who remain Protestant in Chan Kom are small and have little influence. If the one Pat family that still remains in Chan Kom should leave the village, the new religion would, I think, come to an end there and would not revive without a new missionary effort from outside. Yet the effects of the past missionary effort upon the community are in a larger sense permanent; the change is really irreversible. In the wider political world in which the leaders of the village now conduct its affairs—in the scores of settlements making up this and neighboring *municipios*—Protestants are established, and the religious difference is a continuing factor in the political process.

And in the private and local public life of the individual religion has a significance now which will remain indefinitely. Religion is now a matter to talk about, to take into practical consequence, to think over. Visitors come as Protestants or as Catholics. The advantages or merits of the two religions are still discussed. A man now takes a position with regard to his religion. Points of practice are seen in relation to one of the two cults, one of two associations of people. A Protestant will not have the effigy of a saint in his house, nor will any candle burn on his domestic altar. Don Eus, who first found the Bible interesting and good, has been heard to say in recent years that "ordinary people can't be trusted with the Bible." He does not regard himself as ordinary, but he does not read his Bible any more.

VI

The Old Ways and the New

THE retreat to Catholicism occurred as a part of a general return to a more traditional manner of life. The adoption of Protestantism coincides with the period of greatest enthusiasm for change in Chan Kom. The new religion was associated with skepticism about the old ways and with the technical and political advancement of the community. The years 1930–31 marked the apogee of the spirit of progress. Then the ambitions of the people were strongest; then the willingness to make sacrifices for the advancement of the village was greatest; and then the leaders acted most boldly and compellingly.

In those years it seemed that Chan Kom would make a revolution in its manner of life. Men of the community who both before and afterward upheld the traditions of their forefathers were at that time loud in the praise of progress and reason. Then they upheld coeducation and looked with favor on modern dancing in which boy and girl embraced. Those who later spoke against modern dress then allowed their daughters' hair to be cut and bought dresses for them to wear in place of their huipils. With the approval of the leaders, Villa gave a class in the physiology of sex, in which contraception was explained; one man put the knowledge into practice until prevented by his wife's opposition. Urban manners were limited; the Latin embrace was practiced by some; certain young men learned to sing romantic songs; and birthday serenades, in the manner of the Latin town, took place in Chan Kom. Moreover, rationalism and skepticism were in favor. Villa found eager reception for

his talk about science, logic, and human reason. Some of
the most vital beliefs of the people were exposed to criticism. A man who not long before had participated in the
great rain ceremony—and was not long afterward to do so
again—declared in such a discussion that the *cha-chaac* was
worth celebrating simply as a means to entertain and quiet
the people. It was asserted and agreed that the sanctity of
the Cross was but a human invention: what was the Cross
but two sticks with their ordinary relative position slightly
altered? Villa then felt that the secularization of the community was deep and perhaps irreversible.

The change, however, was more apparent than real. To
one who returns to the community in 1948, the conservative temper of the people is apparent. No radical change in
viewpoint has occurred. The bold and critical talk of 1930
is now not to be heard. Today the visitor listens to leaders
who speak with satisfaction of the old religion, and who
deplore the more extreme changes in costume and custom.
The radicalism that prevailed seventeen years ago is for-
gotten or ignored. It may be supposed that that outspoken
radicalism in part depended on the leadership which Villa
gave to it until he left the village in 1931. Also, I think, it
was no more than a superficial expression. Below the words
of skepticism rested a faith that was not really shaken. Behind the talk about the practical utility of the rain ceremony lay the fact that soon after the return to Catholicism
the practice of the pagan ritual was resumed and has been
continued ever since.

The persistence of the cult of pagan origin throughout
the years of religious conflict is attested by brief accounts
given by Villa when he visited the village in 1935 and by
the fuller statements made to us in 1948 with regard to the
entire period of seventeen years. The major ceremony of
this cult, the rain ceremony (*cha-chaac*), was performed by
the people of Chan Kom on July 20, 1935; it was held once

in 1946 and twice in 1947; and in many of the summers between 1935 and 1946. The ceremony (*u hanli col*) in which the individual *milpero* gives thanks to the spirits of the forest and field and makes his prayers for a good harvest has been made many times in Chan Kom in recent years; dates and names of *milperos* and of officiating *h-mens* were told us. The ceremony made in connection with the moving of beehives was held recently in two appropriate cases. And the ceremony (*loh*) by which sickness or other evils are removed or averted from field, corral, settlement, or sick person has been many times performed. First-fruit ceremonies are also continued. The people replied to inquiries about the ceremony held when a house is built (*u chuyenil na*) that that ceremony is no longer performed; and they stated that the two rituals supervised by the *h-men* and performed in connection with the bull fights and dancing at the patronal festival (*dza akab* and *hadz pach*) are well known in Chan Kom and performed in X-Kopteil and X-Kalakdzonot but not in Chan Kom. These replies are just the replies that were received seventeen years ago; these three ceremonies are no more obsolescent in Chan Kom now than they were then. So far as the older people of the village are concerned, the evidence indicates that the entire "pagan" part of the traditional ways of life is maintained with unabated devotion.

It is the *h-men* who today, as seventeen years ago, plays the important role in maintaining the religious tradition. The particular shaman priest whose services are today most commonly employed is an active leader, explaining to the people the religious as well as the practical significance of the ceremonies. Two other *h-mens*, one resident in Chan Kom itself, also have much to do. On one occasion, during the short period of the recent observations, one of these men was so busy answering professional calls that the ceremonial needs of leading men of Chan Kom went for a time

unattended—the *h-men* could not find time to do everything that was asked of him. The seriousness with which
the activities of this kind of sacred professional are still
regarded is evidenced by the fact that in 1944, when the
son of an old *h-men* of the region (who led many a ceremony
performed at the time when the earlier study of Chan Kom
was made) assumed the practice of his own and his father's
calling, the traditional ceremony of purification and initia-
tion (*u lohol h-men*) was performed at a settlement near
Chan Kom, and many of the Chan Kom people contributed food or services.

The *h-men*, with his special knowledge and his opportunities for reflection and discussion of matters of ritual
and belief, continues to reinforce the traditional faith. The
faith is one faith, in which saint and woodland spirit, God
and rain-god, are harmoniously conceived in a single system. "We should go on in the old way," declared one older
man. "To realize the good things that the old people
(*antiguos*) have done, we must follow the ways they have
shown us. Then God, the apostles and the yuntzils [a general word for the spirits of the sky, forest, and field] will not
desert us." The leading *h-men* explained to men of the village that at one time the chief of the rain-gods (*yum chaac*)
was "the most devil of all the devils," but then he knelt
before God and asked his pardon, when God said, "Now
you will serve my kingdom," and gave him two weapons
(lightning and the obsidian blades found in the bush),
which, serving God's kingdom, he ever since has used
against snakes and evil winds for the protection of the
Maya. And recently this same *h-men*, during one of those
long periods of waiting which occur in the ceremonies, told
the men who were participating a version of a fragment of
mythology that combined elements of both traditions with
details of association not present in such narratives as I
have heard them in earlier years. He said that a very long

time ago the waters used to rise out of the cenotes and flood the land, drowning animals and destroying milpa. Then the snake known as *x-chayi* would with its forked tail stop the nostrils of men and women and destroy them. And the *chac-mool*, great feline, smelling the milk of lactating women, would eat their breasts. And, at the "eating of the sun" (eclipse), the hammocks, benches, and other domestic utensils came alive and ate their masters. Christ had not yet come; God had not yet made his *loh* over the earth. But then God passed over the land, making his *loh*, and everything became quiet and at peace.

So is the *loh* ceremony identified with the blessing of God (or Christ). It is "a showing" (*ejemplo*) to the *yuntzils* that they must help men and animals, and live at peace. The *yuntzils*, the pagan supernaturals, are seen as a part, a subordinated part, of that single hierarchy of unseen beings who are addressed in both novena and rain ceremony. Don Eus, establishing out in the bush a settlement for his cattle and his poultry, and an occasional residence for himself and his family, made the *loh* ceremony there with the feeling that he did God's will. He obeyed the instruction of the *h-men* not to move any of the cut stones of the ancient ruin he found at this place, convenient as it would have been to him to make use of them in building his corral; this was the abiding place of the *alux*, certain supernaturals associated with the *yuntzils*. At the same time he noted with satisfaction the red flowers and plants with red leaves at the site he had chosen for the new settlement, for these were signs of the passing of the wounded Christ when, fleeing his pursuers, he made the first blessing on this land, a blessing recalled and renewed in the *loh* ceremony now performed by the *h-men*. And when he and his sons remove their hats as they pass the heaped-up stones the *h-men* has placed at each of the four corners of Don Eus' new domain, it is because the cross that surmounts the stones is sacred, and it

is also because above the stones hovers unseen the protecting *yuntzil*, the *balam*, whose obsidian armament the *h-men*
has placed for him beneath the stones. The religious faith is
one faith, and, in spite of the rise of commerce, the growing
experience with the city, and the appearance of Protestantism, it is substantially unchanged.

Nevertheless, there is a change. Maintained though it is
under the influence and authority of the village leaders who
carry it on with enthusiasm renewed since they turned
back from Protestantism, the religion is maintained in spite
of the presence of some who do not fully believe. Where
before the conduct of the religious life was as unreflecting
and inevitable as sunrise or spring, it is now purposeful; it
is now a thing defended.

"To the west there are many who do not believe." While
the east and the south are associated, in the minds of the
people, with the old ways, "the very Maya," the west is associated with the towns, the *dzul*, and the unbelieving. The
Chan Kom people know more of the west than they used to
know. They travel to the west; they visit the towns. And
among the new settlers in Chan Kom are some who came
from villages in that territory where the *cha-chaac* is not
performed or is performed in the presence of only a few
laughable old men. A Chan Kom man talked about this.
"Out there the poor people see and hear the *dzules* laughing
at these things; they see what the *dzules* do, and they fancy
that that is what is right. They say, 'Take out *zaca* [the
ritual cornmeal]? Better drink it myself.' Here in Chan
Kom we shall lose these things if many such people come to
live among us."

We were, however, unable to find any open skeptics
among these new residents. We did not talk much with
them. I can only report that no one of them showed his
doubts to us. One man, an old man who has lived in a town,
was reported as frankly skeptical of the old rituals, and the

city-dwelling mother of a Chan Kom resident, who visits
the village occasionally, does not hesitate to show her sense
of detachment from these village customs. But at recent
ceremonies several of the newcomers from the western villages have attended. Their influence is not yet important.
It is enough to make the pious village leaders a little self-
conscious. One of them tried to put into words his view of
the undeniable fact that there are people who do not believe, as well as many who do. "It is like having a telescope
[microscope]. There are two kinds of believing; each has its
way of seeing: the way of seeing with the microscope, and
the way of seeing the *alux*."

And then there are the young people. Some of them do
not have faith in the pagan rituals. I know this only because some of the older people tell us so and from the fact
that some of the young people with whom we talked about
the ceremonies showed a reluctance to discuss the topic,
which I took to arise from their own uncertainty of attitude. These are the young men who have most education
and who go often to the city. Some of them belong to Protestant families. What can be asserted with confidence is
that the disbelieving young people do not yet publicly assert their disbelief in the religious rituals. They attend the
rain ceremony, all of them, even the most city-wise. No
conflict between old and young as to religious faith was reported or suggested in anything we heard; I do not think
that there is as yet any such. If there is, it shows forth privately, within the family.

The ceremonies which have a strong practical significance, which are precautionary or therapeutic rather than
religious, do provide cases, reported to me, of expressed differences in belief. The influence of the younger generation
in developing doubt of the traditional ways appears in
these cases. With the growth of the cattle industry, and the
knowledge the villagers have of the existence of hoof-and-

mouth disease in other parts of the Republic, there has developed a lively interest in the sicknesses of cattle. The government has tried to spread widely a knowledge of protection of cattle by injection of scientific preventives. On the other hand, the traditional way of protecting cattle is to perform the *loh* ceremony at the lands where the cattle feed and are corraled. "Which procedure gives better protection?" is the main question the cattle-owner asks himself, in spite of the teaching of the *h-men* that the *loh* ceremony is God's blessing, and so a religious duty as well as a wise precaution. Two older men, kinsmen, discussed what to do when their cattle began dying. The married son of one of them, city-wise, urged his father to have his cattle injected; the man was convinced and tried to persuade his kinsmen to take advantage of the coming of the veterinary to the village. But the other man said he did not trust the hypodermic injections; he would have *loh* made. The first man brought the veterinary, who injected his cattle. Nevertheless, several died. Then, when cattle of the other man began to die, this man had *loh* made, and, no more of his cattle dying, he felt his choice of remedies vindicated. And now his kinsman, persuaded by these events, had *loh* made at his corral also. Nevertheless this man's son remained unconvinced; he did not join in the preparations for the *loh* ceremony at the corral where he and his father kept their cattle, and those which he owns he himself injected according to methods he learned from a veterinary.

The choice between *loh* and hypodermic in protecting cattle in Chan Kom is, at the time of this reporting, in uncertain balance. The choice is influenced partly by observations of effectiveness, real or supposed, of the two preventives. "Many hogs die in Valladolid, where they do not make *loh*." The arguments of science are not unheard but may take turns unexpected by their advocates. Don Eus, reading an educational sheet distributed by federal agrar-

ian authorities, was convinced by an article as to the evils
of deforestation. But an article reporting limited success in
controlling hoof-and-mouth disease he read as further evidence that modern methods are unavailing to meet this
danger. "They should have made *loh* in the first place."
And the *loh* ceremony has powerful support in its connection with religion and with the views of nature held in the
village. When the *h-men*, brought to deal with sickness of
cattle, walks across the land, watching the knolls, the trees,
the mounds where the *alux* hide, looks into his crystal to
see what the supernaturals are doing, and then announces
that the *yuntzils* are "talking strong" and that three of the
balams at Ticincacab and one *yuntzil* of the well require
propitiation, he seems to say what the landowner has always known, in a general way, about his land and the
beings that inhabit it. And the ceremony, when performed,
with its two altars (one for the evil winds), the sacrificed
poultry, the dish of turkey meat, and the bottle of brandy,
the ceremony in which participate the cattle-owner's entire
family and some of his friends, has the authority of a collective expressive effort of all the interested parties. To bring
out some *dzul* to prick the cattle with a needle is not the
same thing at all.

Perhaps it is nearer the truth to say that no definite
choice between old and new remedy is made. Rather, the
new is added to the old. If one does not work, the other is
tried. This is certainly the impression which arises from
what was told us about the treatment of sickness in human
beings. There is in Chan Kom much more knowledge of the
city man's medicines than there was in 1931. At that time
only one man was an enthusiastic user of store-bought
remedies and of hypodermic injections. Now these remedies are generally known and widely used. The cultural
mission, as remarked before, taught several young women
to use the hypodermic needle; the mission brought a drug

case to the village, and a member of the mission with some nurse's training promoted the use of these remedies. The stores of Chan Kom now sell many medicines, some patent, some standard, and many others are bought in the city. There is knowledge of penicillin, and several of the villagers have taken this remedy in the city. Nevertheless, the traditional methods of healing are much employed. I do not think they are, for most people, displaced. They are supplemented by modern remedies. A woman who knows much herbal medicine has many calls a week from patients; there are other herbalists in the village about whose practice I did not learn. The *h-mens* are busy curing sickness, of the city-wise as of the less sophisticated, of Protestants as well as of Catholics. Two of the younger men who go much to the city have not used the *h-men* in recent years; one of these, that man who prefers the veterinary to the *loh* ceremony, did not call the *h-men*, although he lost two children by sickness. This young man is, I think, the most nearly convinced that the treatment of the *h-men* are not effective.

For most people a persisting sickness means now a trying of successive remedies. A woman with an infected breast is treated for days with herbal remedies; the condition does not improve, and her husband calls the *h-men*. If he fails, she may go to the city. But the city is still far away and is a dangerous place. In other cases reported us, the *h-men* is called after the city remedy has been tried, and some of the older people tell with satisfaction of case after case where the *h-men* brought about a cure after urban remedies had failed. A mother with an epileptic son takes him from curer to curer, in whatever order opportunity provides. An older woman with an abscessed infected tooth, having tried herbal remedies easily available, is uncertain whether to go to the city and face its difficulties and dangers or to call a powerful *h-men*. When her husband tries unsuccessfully to bring the *h-men*, and her sufferings are great, she resigns herself to die, and her husband talks to her throughout the night, helping her to face death, talking to her of its inevitability.

Yet the general impression to be reported is that people are less easily resigned to die while they are more troubled about how to live. A sickness has a more varied and a less self-consistent course than was once the case, when one called the *h-men*, did what he told with the conviction born of the fact that his way was the only way, and got well or did not. Now one may choose this course or that, this remedy before the other or after it. There is no clear point at which one has done all that one can and must leave the event in the hands of God.

There is one special class of circumstances which tends to eliminate traditional ritual. This is the situation in which a new physical object, or new technique, displaces an old one. Then it is apparently an easy assumption for the people to make that the new object "does not need" the ceremony. So, in 1931, the ceremony made by the *h-men* to purify a new house was disappearing as people began to build their houses of masonry. For the masonry house the ceremony of the *h-men*, with its burying of certain ritual plants and its recognition of the crosses formed by the intersecting poles, was inappropriate; and in the town people who build masonry houses may call the priest to bless the house. The blessing by the priest came to be associated with the masonry house, and the *u chuyenil na* became infrequent. Similarly, the introduction into Chan Kom, since 1931, of "American" (Italian?) bees, which are kept in boxes, did not bring about an extension of the traditional ceremonies performed in establishing or moving the old-style beehive of hollow logs inhabited by the native bees; it was felt that the new hives "did not need the ceremony." Something of the same process is involved when, as now happens, a tract of land is persistingly cultivated, and it is said that "that land does not need *u hanli col.*" On the other hand, some newly introduced objects are associated with established categories. It appears that the honey from the new kind of bee is "cold," where honey from the native bee has long been recognized as "hot." But this is a case in which the important traditional view of the people is that *all* comestibles belong to one or the other of these metaphysical yet practical categories ("cold" or "hot"). So, when a man ate the new honey when he was overheated from work, and felt ill, he was at once assured by those who had never thought of the matter before, probably, that the new honey must be "cold"—so "cold" it injured him when he ate it when he was in a hot condition. Such accidents of experience and interpretation suggest how it comes about that there are many local variations in the lists of "hot" and "cold" objects.

On the whole, and without important exception that we could discover, the people's view of the world around them is unchanged. It is inhabited by the same beings and within it lie the same dangers that characterized it seventeen years ago. Men go down into wells as they went down into cenotes, and the well, like the cenote, is an uncanny place, an opening into hidden places of the earth, a lurking place of snake and evil wind. When a snake was recently seen at the bottom of an unfinished well, its appearance was at once connected with a flight of hornets, the dying of dogs placed at the well to guard property left there, and the sickness of cattle feeding there. The evil winds were loosed from the well and from the body of the snake. After the snake had been carefully removed, the well-digger would proceed only when smoking a cigarette, for tobacco is traditionally used to protect one from snakes. Some of the men most literate and town-wise shared in these doings and attitudes. The *uay-cot*, a merchant with power to fly on mat wings by night and enter storehouses unseen, there to seize the property that mysteriously appears in his store, is real today, although men of Chan Kom are now themselves storekeepers. The *uay-cots* are in other villages and towns. The other kinds of *uayes*, those human beings who by night transform themselves into dogs or cows, still occur in Chan Kom. Principal young citizens of the village went to their doors one night in 1948. Aroused by the barking of domestic dogs, they were just in time to see the supernatural black bitch, with pendant breasts, pass running across the plaza. Mention of one such story brings many others, told in all seriousness, and the literate and the town-wise take equal part with the others. Talk of the *uayes* leads to a recounting of an adventure had just last week with a *x-tabai*, a spirit in woman's form, who mounted the horse of a merchant on his way to the village and would not let him go until he recited a prayer. At another informal gathering in one of the village stores, I take up a small clay head that was found in a milpa, and a villager says at once that that is the head of an *alux* and points out the hole in the head where the soul of the *alux* enters and makes it come alive. He remarks that he saw one of these beings, animated, a few years ago at Ticimul and tells of the experience in some detail. Another tells a similar story, and a third remarks that there are not so many *alux* as there once were. So, too, a man will say that "not so many people turn themselves into *uayes* as once did." But nothing of disbelief as to such matters appears.

The conceptions as to the causes of sickness appear to continue much as they were in 1931. Although some instruction was given to the people of Chan Kom at that time in the germ theory of disease by teachers and visitors, and although the cultural mission of 1944–45 strove to improve the understanding of the people as to scientific ideas of health and hygiene, in this visit to the village in 1948 I heard nothing from the people about microbes and infections. A suggestion that colds pass by contagion was met by expressions of amusement. The far-extending idea of "evil winds"—semipersonified unseen airs that carry sickness—is, plainly, as generally known and as undoubted as it was. The conceptions as to disturbance of health from unwise combinations of "hot" and "cold" substances, mentioned above, are also met with as frequently as before. And one of the most literate of the men of the village, having cut his finger, was careful to put honey on the wound before going near his menstruating wife, lest the *kinam*—the dangerous force attending women in their menses—might enter his wound and make him sick. Nor would this man go to a wake with his wounded finger, for a corpse too has its *kinam*.

Concerning the treatment of pregnant women and of newborn children so little was learned at this visit that no comparison can be made with the knowledge and practices of 1931. Questioning of two of the men in the village who might have learned something about birth control brought the conclusion that nothing is known about it and that these men have not been thinking about it. The greater number of living children is a matter of comment, and there is some concern mixed with pride in such a remark as: "Now when the land gives less corn than it did there are so many children to be fed." The attendant at all births in Chan Kom is a daughter of a *h-men*, a midwife practicing according to traditional methods; she speaks no Spanish and knows nothing of the practices of the town.

Since the return to the traditional religion, all children are baptized by a priest except those born in the families that remained Protestant. The children born in families that returned to Catholicism are likewise taken to the priest. But in the case of one child born during the period of Protestant conversion, baptism was postponed with the result that the priest has now refused to baptize until the child should take instruction. There is some reason to suppose that there is less haste in carrying the child to the distant priest than there once was; several children, already walking, were reported as not yet baptized, and the traditional view that the child should be baptized before the fontanelle closes was described as something "the old people did." The traditional manner of finding names for children—choosing among the names of the saints according to the Catholic calendar—is on the whole followed, but a few departures from custom have appeared. An old man let his youngest—and probably last—child be baptized in the usual way with the name of a saint of the day of the birth and later asked the civil registrar if the name could be changed to his own given name. It was done, and the child is known by his father's name. Inspection of the list of recently registered given names shows only two that are not saints' names, and these two occur in the family of the very city-wise young man, whose wife was brought up in a town. The selection of "pretty" names (as flower names for girls in place of saints' names) is a declared association with the ways of the town. This same family may be one in which the ancient ceremony of *hetz mek* is not practiced; we did not find out. The general statement is made with an air of confidence that this ceremony of aboriginal origin— in which the infant is, when first carried astride the hip, assured a good development of its faculties—is made "for all the children in Chan Kom" or "is made now more than ever." And indeed in a dozen or so cases into which we inquired we found only one in which the performance of the ceremony was not confirmed by the details as to sponsor and approximate time of performance of the ritual. One boy, son of a man for whose many other children the ceremony had not been performed, had had no *hetz mek* made for him, and his odd manner of walking was explained by this neglect. *Hetz mek* is made for children of Protestant families too. Even more impressive, as a persistence of traditional domestic rituals, is the frequent celebration of that ceremony (*poh kab, tzicil*) wherein the parents of a baptized child kneel and wash the hands of those *compadres* who held their child at the font. This ceremony was performed in at least two instances in 1948, in literate and town-wise families. On the other hand, the most sophisticated young married man in the village has not performed the ceremony for his *compadres*.

Information was obtained as to ten marital unions established in Chan Kom in the six years immediately preceding the winter of 1948. (These were not all the unions that were formed during that period.) In five of the ten cases the marriages were preceded by the usual traditional negotiations between representatives of the two families concerned, with the customary culmination in delivery of the bride gifts (*muhul*), and were solemnized in the domestic ceremonies that occur just before the bride and groom begin living together. In short, they were fully "old-style" marriages. They represented the norm as it was in Chan Kom a generation ago and as it is still conceived. According to this ideal the girl, a virgin, has had little communication, if any, with the bridegroom (or with any other man); the parents on both sides make the formal arrangements for the marriage without participation by boy or girl; the ceremonies place on the union the approval of the two families and express their decision to become connubially linked. This was the ideal that did in fact find expression in five of the ten cases. In three of these the bridegrooms were among the most town-wise of the young men of Chan Kom. Witnessing the delivery of the bride-gifts that sealed the contract of marriage between one young storekeeper and a girl of the village this winter was an experience convincing as to the sincerity and piety which still attends this ritual solemnization of a familially arranged marriage.

But Chan Kom has long known and recognized unions of "runaway" lovers. Occasionally, at the time of the first study of the village, a boy and a girl would begin living together in the village, in spite of parental opposition, or would go off together for a time and then return. Unfortunately, precise information as to the frequency of such unions at that time is lacking. My impression is that these unions are becoming commoner. Of the ten recent unions immediately under consideration, three or four were of this sort. In three cases a girl, who might otherwise have claimed a *muhul* and a traditional wedding, began living with a boy against her parents' wish. In all three cases the parents soon or at last condoned the act and accepted the arrangement. In such a case a marriage by traditional familial ceremony would be regarded as quite inappropriate. In one case, after long discussion centering around the suitability of such action, the couple was later married by civil registry; in the other two cases they were not. The fourth case of union accomplished outside of familial arrangements in recent years was one in which a girl got herself a bad reputation as having had sexual relationships with more than one man; when an older man decided to live maritally with her, he merely began to do so; no one would in such a case suggest solemnization of the union. The girl who conspicuously loses her virginity and the girl who runs away with her lover "do not deserve *muhul*."

The tenth of these cases deserves reporting in some detail, for it shows an attempt to realize the ideal marriage in spite of circumstances which, in the native view, might well have made the rituals inappropriate. A girl of Chan Kom became pledged to marry a boy of another village; the two families entered into the customary engagements, but *muhul* had not yet been delivered. In this intermediate stage, before the pledges of agreement to marry had been made, the girl decided that she preferred a boy of Chan Kom. At just this time political enmity between the other village in which the first boy lived and Chan Kom was at its most intense. The father of the girl and the father of the boy now preferred by the girl found it easy to agree that the old incomplete engagement should be broken and an engagement made between the two young people of Chan Kom. But then the girl's parents learned the girl was pregnant by the boy of the other village. They told the parents of the Chan Kom boy, and all four discussed what should be done. It was agreed that, as the girl was not a virgin, no marriage ceremony was really deserved. On the other hand, the two Chan Kom families were eager to enter into connubial connection. They decided—somewhat as Huck Finn and Jim decided it would be wrong to steal persimmons— that, although a marriage by priest or register would be improper, they would have the traditional rituals of marriage. In shortened form the delivery of *muhul* was accomplished, and the domestic marriage rituals were then held, in the customary way, at the house of the girl's parents. With some hope of success, the two families thus sought to represent the marriage as one which had come about as if the interrupted negotiations with the boy from outside the village had not occurred. "To have no ceremonies would be a bad example for the younger children," said one of the parents. It was possible for them to realize in substance the social values of an old-style marriage, because the first would-be bridegroom was an outsider to the village, because the people of Chan Kom were hostile to this village, and because the fact of the pregnancy was not generally known.

In none of these cases was the question of marriage by a priest or by registry a principal question. As was true in earlier years, marriage by a priest is valued but is something of an "extra" among rituals that validate a union and contribute to the prestige of families. Marriage through the civil registry is thought to be desirable for the public sanction of the union which it implies and for the legal rights which it is understood such registry establishes. Yet, during the period of the recent observations some misunderstanding of the national law making young men from eighteen to twenty-five years of age liable to military service had caused the people of Chan Kom to believe that the civil registrar was forbidden to record the marriages of men of such age. So in their cases no entry in the registry was made. The people criticized the misunderstood law as bad in interfering with a proper element of "good" marriages. But to leave out civil registry is a small matter compared with omitting *muhul* and the solemn ceremony of marriage which takes place according to native tradition—these are the rituals which chiefly dignify that marriage which meets the ideal.

The principal conclusion to which one comes in considering changes in the ideas and the practices as to marriage in Chan Kom in these seventeen years is, then, that the older people think of a "good marriage" today as they thought of it in 1931, and that the young people, while they probably depart increasingly in practice from this ideal, do not deny the ideal. There is no revolt of the younger generation in matters of marriage and family life any more than in matters of religion. In one of the ten cases the question of forbidden degree of kinship arose out of the strong desire of a young man to marry his father's brother's granddaughter. The struggle arose, not between father and son or between father and daughter, but between the two fathers (uncle and nephew), and the insistence of the girl's father brought the match to consummation. The priest, in the town, pronounced the union sinful and refused to marry the couple, and the *h-men* as vigorously advised against the marriage as sinful from his viewpoint. The marriage was nevertheless consummated. When misfortune followed upon the marriage, it convinced the girl's father that he should not have allowed it. And due largely to the influence which the unfortunate outcome of this union exercised over the views of people, a proposed marriage between young people similarly related was, soon afterward, prevented. So far as very limited information suggests, the views of the people as to choice of spouse are little changed. No information was obtained as to marriage with a deceased wife's sister; no case occurred in recent years.

On the other hand, there is a little evidence that some young people not only are disposed to choose their own mates more freely than was true before but also that they tend to cast a wider look in making the choice. In one of the ten cases of marriage which were well reported, the young man asserted strongly to his father his wish to marry a girl who had lived long in a city and who had come to Chan Kom with her family on an extended visit. Here the young man was asserting his claim to identify himself with the values of the city as against his father's views that a "good marriage" is made with a "hard-working" girl of the villages. The father's reluctance was overcome by the son, and the marriage was effected. It ended in divorce—the only divorce to occur in Chan Kom, according to what was told us, in these seventeen years. But when the young man remarried, he chose another girl from a town, with town clothes and some town manners. The resulting household is accepted by the people, but it is not regarded by older people as a good sort of marriage, because the wife does not perform some of the hard work that Maya women perform. A report that a boy of the village was arranging to marry a much more citified girl, daughter of a schoolteacher, as already mentioned in chapter iv, was strongly criticized for the disparity between the two ways of life which it implied. One older man said, "I don't want my son to marry a *xunan* (a woman of the city; not a Maya). She will get sick, or the children will, and she wouldn't be

able to do the hard work. She would just go to the movies."
And the two young men who chose town-bred wives are
still very exceptional among young men of Chan Kom;
most young people would accept the parental view. On the
other hand, from several sources came statements to the
effect that "the young people care more for blonde sweet-
hearts than they used to." And: "It used to be that all that
was necessary in a sweetheart was that she be healthy, industrious, and good-tempered. Now the blondes are much
wanted." One man said that he noticed that more blonde
girls were being born, apparently in response to the changing demand. "It seems the race is changing." The superior
value attached to blondeness (by which is meant a degree
less of pigmentation) was present in Chan Kom in 1931;
probably it is more marked now, as an aspect of the disposition of some young people to take over values of the
town and city.

As was the case in 1931, the concern of parents over their
children is greatest in connection with marriage and first
sexual relations, although no particular age is recognized
as an age of difficulty; and I do not think that there is any
concept of adolescence. Parents want their young children
to be obedient and industrious; as they grow older, they
are admonished and watched, the girls that their virginity
may be preserved and their good name as modest and hard-
working young women be kept, and the boys lest a bad
reputation attach to them for idleness, drinking, or pursuit
of women. Nothing was said to me to suggest that any attempt is made now, as none was made before, to instruct
young people in matters of sex; some learn such matters
early by observation and chance information; others learn
little about it until marriage.

Nevertheless, a marked change has taken place in the
behavior of many children and young people, a change
which suggests that children now in school will later act

more freely on their own initiative than is the case among most of the recently married young people of the village today. This change is apparent in a greater readiness to act conspicuously in public and a greater readiness to associate with members of the opposite sex. It is the school that chiefly stimulates this change, although the example of boys and girls of the town and city, seen when the villagers make their now frequent trips to these places, and the example of occasional visitors to the village, supplement the influence of the school. Some of the schoolteachers, during these years, have made strong efforts to change the behavior of the children in these respects, and some of them have taken vigorous positions against the will of the older generation of villagers; it is here where the old way of life and the new have openly joined issue. On the whole, with setbacks, the new ways slowly prevail.

The principal issues have occurred in connection with clothing, organized sports, and coeducation. It has already been reported, in chapter ii, how a schoolteacher attempted to compel all girls in the school to give up the folk costume, adopt dresses of city style, and bob their hair. The reaction to this reform was strong; nevertheless, some girls continued thereafter to dress in town fashion. Daughters of several men who go often to the city have also given up the huipil, as daily attire, in favor of the dress. As remarked in the earlier connection, the assumption of this attire carries with it connotations that affect the habits of the wearer: a dress-wearing girl is less likely to haul firewood (but quite as likely to fetch water), and she probably feels freer to participate in organized play. A type of girl now occurs in Chan Kom, a type not seen there in 1931, a girl who joins with zest in baseball with other girls at the school, who may play a little ball with friends and neighbors, including boys, and who talks about the city and her wish to go there. She speaks up when spoken to and has not the shy, almost voiceless and completely unassertive, manner that prevailed among young women in former generations. Only a few such girls there are as yet in Chan Kom, but to a recognizable degree many others act more freely and appear more publicly than was true in 1931. Then women, with hardly an exception, were shy and especially remained secluded if any foreigner to the village was present. Women now stand outside their houses more often than before, though they do not come forward to investigate an event of interest; they leave their houses oftener to view what is going on in the plaza. And they meet visitors with more openness of manner and greater confidence.

This greater freedom of manner of some of the younger women and girls is in part supported by the wider range of activities that are becoming appropriate to women and the opportunities, limited though they yet are, for women to contribute to handicraft production. The embroidering which is traditional is now supplemented, in the cases of some of these women and girls whose men have connections with the city, by crocheting, by the making of both huipils and dresses by hand- and machine-sewing, and by a little knitting (taught in the village this winter by my wife). The wife of one of the sandalmakers helps him to sew the sandals he sells; and the two girls who have learned how to give hypodermic injections probably receive some prestige, as well as money, from the practice of the art. Nevertheless, there is as yet no place for any woman in the public and governmental affairs of the community. (The preparation of festal foods is an obligation, but the work is done privately, in the houses and away from the men.) Women do not join in formal public assemblies, except of course dances and the recently arranged "cultural programs," nor do they come to the municipal building to see what the men are doing. As tradition requires, even the staff that manages the church is composed entirely of men.

That many of the schoolgirls have learned how to play baseball is notable. There are strong sentiments that would prevent their participation in the sport. There is, first, the strong disfavor which attaches to unproductive effort. This sentiment stands in the way of organized play for either boys or girls. Second, there is the strong moral judgment that girls beyond puberty should remain apart, restrained, busy with household tasks, and away from public notice and especially the notice of men and boys. Such a girl, an almost voiceless, dovelike creature, is, in their word of praise, *zuhuy*, a virgin in spirit as in body, aloof and pure. The playing of baseball by girls, still with little exception confined to the school and with supervision and direction of the teacher, violates this principle of conduct; it is no wonder that there is much criticism of baseball by parents of girls.

Baseball is not yet a pastime for girls accepted by the people; it depends on the support and urging of the teachers. But baseball for boys and young men has become established; the younger generation carries it on as an adult sport, now independent of the school. (Why baseball has become so generally popular in rural Yucatan, while basketball and soccer, also introduced through the schools, have not, I cannot say.) More than half of the settlements of the Chan Kom *municipio* have their teams and their baseball diamonds, and many intervillage games are played, usually on Sunday mornings. This has all developed since 1931. The traditional values approve conspicuous public activity by men, and rivalry between villages, in war and politics, is now easily expressed in these contests. On the other hand, the games are not matters of general interest in the village; audiences are desultory and small, and women and girls, consistent with the traditional view of their role, do not feel it appropriate to attend.

There is also criticism of baseball by parents of boys.

The participation of boys and young men in baseball is the most important situation, perhaps the only frequent and much-discussed situation brought about by the entry of new ways of life into Chan Kom, where disagreement between the older and younger generations is manifest. Many mothers and fathers disapprove of the game, because it dirties clothing and makes greater the already onerous task of laundering and because it wastes time. Two of the principal men of the village have forbidden their sons to play baseball; the team must do without the services of an excellent shortstop and a fair pitcher. One of these sons, forbidden to play, is married. But there are other cases where young married sons take part in the play, although their fathers frown on it. No case was told me of an unmarried son, of course living at home, who played the game against his father's will. That degree of filial disobedience is hardly possible in Chan Kom as yet. The argument of waste of time, presented again and again, is strong, for every boy is taught from very early years that hard work and prudent husbandry are the very center of all virtue. One father said to his son: "The priest earns twenty pesos holding a Mass; he does it just by walking back and forth, clean and slow; you boys walk two leagues to X-Calakoop, come back worn and dirty, and earn nothing."

The two virtues, productive industry and the withdrawal of girls from males and masculine affairs, thus meet a threat in the progressive programs of the school. To the people of the village the school is both a good thing and a bad. It brings some changes that are wanted and some that are not. To read and to write are good and to learn to speak Spanish. It is good also to learn a little arithmetic. The occasional teacher who helps the girls to learn how to sew or to cook dishes not known before is praised; and at a time when some instruction in gardening and the care of poultry was given, this, too, was appreciated. On the other hand, the school is often thought of as a place of idleness and, much worse, of the learning of vicious habits. There are teachers who spend hours standing or sitting, while the children are in school studying, thus setting the children an example of idleness. The time spent on play, on games, is regarded as waste by many parents, although others have good to say of the value to health of such exercises. The greatest evil of the school lies, however, for most people in the close association of boys and girls. The teachers are regarded as urging immodesty upon children, especially girls. It is often told that when one of the teachers arranged the seating in the schoolroom, she put a boy beside every girl, and said to each boy, "This is your *novia*." Such things are told with lowered voice. It is an indecency—"a thing of the devil." So the round games, in which children join hands, are disliked by many parents, and the teachers we knew did not insist upon them except when the school inspector came. At the time of these recent observations several families were keeping their children out of school, partly because of their dislike of coeducation, partly because of controversies between them and the teachers on other issues.

In the issues and choices presented by the school, then, the old ways and the new meet at points of conflict. In defining their path to progress, the people of Chan Kom imagined progress as an adoption of certain benefits which the town and the city could provide. They conceived no moral revolution. The benefits they were ready to accept were those which harmonized with the scheme of values, with the ideas of the good life, which they had long held and taken for granted. Where the city offered them something markedly inconsistent with this scheme of life, they felt it to be bad. The traditional values on the whole guide the course of progress in Chan Kom. To a further consideration of those values and their influence on social change, the eighth chapter will be devoted.

VII

The Road to the Light

AS THE language of progress, the tongue which the native must use to communicate with the town and city, Spanish has long been highly valued in Chan Kom. According to the census, that part of the population of the village which speaks Spanish increased from 14 per cent in 1930 to 53 per cent in 1940. (In 1930 twenty-six males and nine females, in a population of 251, were reported as speaking Spanish. In 1940 eighty-two males and sixty-five females, out of a population of 270, were so reported.) The later census has probably been generous in including as Spanish-speaking some individuals whose knowledge of the language is rudimentary. In 1948, eight years later, these figures still seem to me too high. The men whose judgment on the question I trust expressed the opinion that today about half the boys and men can carry on a conversation in understandable Spanish and that something less than half the girls and women can do so. A list was given me of only nine adult women who could speak Spanish fairly well; some of these certainly do not speak it really well. Still, the increase in knowledge of the language since 1930 is very considerable. For this the school is the principal cause: almost all the older children and young married men, and some married women, can speak some Spanish; one or two speak the language easily and fairly well. There are a few residents who came to Chan Kom from other settlements where they learned Spanish as their first language.

The use of Spanish by a villager may be necessary in talking with a teacher, a trader, or a representative of the

outside government. Even if such an outsider can address
the villager in Maya, use of Spanish in such a situation
puts the villager in a position of advantage. At once it suggests that he is instructed, enlightened—that he is no ig-
norant rustic. Furthermore, knowledge of Spanish is very
desirable in assuming positions of leadership, and it is almost essential, today, in one taking the position of municipal president or justice of the peace. A man who did not
talk Spanish might take one of these positions, but he is
far less likely to do so than one who does speak Spanish.
Spanish is the preferred language of formal and public
occasions. A leader will make an address to all the people
in Maya, for only in this language can he reach them all
and only in Maya is he likely to be fluent; on the other
hand, the municipal president, conducting an inquiry in
the "Municipal Palace" in the necessary Maya is likely to
use Spanish in giving a loud and peremptory order to a
constable.

Maya is, then, still the overwhelmingly common speech,
the language of domestic and informal affairs. In almost
every family, when old and young are together, talking,
Maya alone is used. When the children leave the schoolroom,
they drop at once into Maya for their play. Two or three
of the families that have come in recent years to settle in
Chan Kom came from settlements on the highway where
Spanish was the language of everyday intercourse; the children of these families are learning Maya, as a second language, from their playfellows. On the other hand, as almost all these playfellows can speak some Spanish, some
Spanish is heard in play groups, as was not the case in
1931. The terms used in baseball are English; so it comes
about that a combination of three languages will be heard
when the boys or young men play that game. This is practically all the English that is known; the baseball terms are
hardly thought of as English by those who use them.

A striking expression of the value placed on Spanish, and of the determination of some parents that their children speak Spanish, is the fact, which I hesitated to record until I had made very sure of its truth: in several households the children learned Spanish before they learned Maya, in spite of the general use of Maya among children and in the community generally. These parents took pains to speak only Spanish to their children in the home. In two families (and possibly in others) small children speak Spanish, and not Maya, although the mother speaks very little Spanish. The father accomplished this result with the aid of Spanish-speaking older children of his own and neighboring families. These children are actually learning Maya as a second language, and, in one case, the father being dead, the Spanish-speaking child communicates with its surviving parent through the few Spanish words she knows and through the other children of the household.

Although some little use of Maya is made in the school in the first steps toward literacy, Spanish alone is the language of the written and printed word. An outsider, a Maya-valuing *dzul*, might put up a sign in the Indian language; it would not occur to a native of the village to do so; the first signboard in Chan Kom—a price list and notice about terms as to grinding corn—is in Spanish, in a household where the older people speak no Spanish. All the literature available to the people is in Spanish.

In the form in which I have them, the statistics as to literacy according to the censuses of 1930 and 1940 are not quite comparable: in 1930, 39 per cent of those ten years of age or over were reported as literate; in 1940, 43 per cent of the total population was so reported. The figures do not tell us very much, anyway. Of the persons reported as literate in 1930, sixteen were reported as not speaking Spanish! I should say that there are today several score of adults who can read simple Spanish with good understanding;

there are only a few who can read a newspaper or a New Testament with understanding. I do not think that more than half-a-dozen women can do so. The number of men who can write Spanish with some proficiency and accuracy must be very small; very few men are qualified to serve as civil registrar. It is the children who learn to read and write, and it is the school that teaches them. The national campaign to reduce illiteracy among adults was not a success in Chan Kom; the teacher in Chan Kom at the time of the campaign was not liked by some of the Chan Kom people, and real difficulties or assumed excuses frustrated the effort to teach the illiterate adults to read and write.

The principal use of literacy is to communicate formal information, as was the case in 1931. Many communications from offices of state or national government now arrive in Chan Kom, by mail, and not a few must be answered. The civil registrar, of course, enters his official records in blank books provided by the government. The hearing of a criminal charge or legal claim requires the making of official documents. Besides this increase of the use of literacy, for such official purposes, there is an increase of personal mail. Several letters of private correspondence arrive every week, and several go.

Chan Kom is more familiar with books than it was in 1931. At that time Villa and I reported only two books in common use: the calendar, in which names were looked up for newborn children, and little books of Spanish prayers. Such books, again providing formal information, are still needed and used in Chan Kom. But today many more books are owned, and some of them are occasionally read. The reading of the New Testament, by the Protestants, has been mentioned more than once in these pages; it is read as part of their ritual, and a few people read it to see what it says. The school has provided many more readers than one could have seen in the village in 1931, and many of these have found their way into homes. Occasionally some literate young person will read such a reader aloud to other members of the family. Their material consists chiefly of descriptive accounts of episodes of rural life, in many cases moral in tone, or of paragraphs or poems expressing sentiments of national patriotism. In addition to such readers, there are a few families who own other books: one has an elementary book on the English language (unused), an elementary geography, and an elementary hygiene. A book on child care reported years ago in one household has disappeared. In some households there are books having to do with needlework; these are much valued for the pictorial designs they offer as examples for the embroidery of the women especially. Most of the people make no use of books at all, except as the children are required to open books in the school.

The books, then, as the written documents, on the whole add to the technical knowledge. They do little to suggest new values, standards, or worlds of the imagination. The schoolbooks contain little poetic imagination or humor; they lack realistic information too. They contain, on the whole, "set pieces"; there is little to capture the interest. People who want to learn something about how to raise poultry, to crochet, or to speak a few words of English may seek another sort of book, a technical book, that will tell them how; it is doubtful if most of them can make very much use of the books for such ends when they get them. And, as providing a content of culture to the lives of the people, the printed pages that are available to the people of Chan Kom are almost entirely barren. Only the Bible, in so far as it is read and thought about by a very few, and the sixth-grade reader that Don Eus has received as a gift from a city person—as Don Eus reads it, with a mind that is truly inquiring and speculative and rational—are there, so far as I know, to enlarge the horizons of the mind.

The newspaper deserves special mention. The city paper began to appear occasionally in Chan Kom at the time of the earlier observations. With more frequent contact with the city, and the spread of rural schools in the neighborhood, more copies of this paper have come to Chan Kom. The town-wise young man of Chan Kom, mentioned more than once in these pages, for a time subscribed to this paper. No one in Chan Kom does so now. It would be an expense a villager would find hard to justify. Many of the teachers of the region receive a city newspaper through the mail; it is not read regularly by anybody in Chan Kom. We never saw either of the two young men who go oftenest to the city to make purchases for the store reading a newspaper in the village. On the other hand, there are two or three other men who occasionally read such copies of the city paper as reach Chan Kom. Don Eus is, of course, one of these. He reads articles on national or even on foreign news and tries to ponder their significance. He has learned how to find in the newspaper the reports of the price of corn on the Chicago Board of Trade and has observed that the market price in Merida is responsive to these quotations; he applies this information to his own decisions as to buying or selling corn. He reads also the informational or propaganda papers published and sent out by offices of the state government; these deal with agrarian or political matters. The knowledge that other people in Chan Kom have of the matters reported or urged in these papers comes to them largely as Don Eus, having read the paper, explains the contents as the men sit together in the plaza in the evening.

Here may be reported the expressed judgment of this man as to the value of books. Don Eus has formed the opinion that it is not enough just to learn to read: one must make use of books. He observes that, although the children and some of the adults have learned to read in Chan Kom, they do not make use of books. On the other hand, he says, it is not clear to him that one is always better off for reading books. He notes that in the city, where there are so many books, there are also many troubles. "In the city people are always talking about their problems, wondering how to solve them. Out here, even if we do not use books, we have some way to solve every difficulty. In the old days, there could have been no books, and yet people knew what to do in every situation." It seems to him that, although books are there to help one solve problems, where there are many books, there also are many problems. Nevertheless, he continues to read, and, when printed matter along the lines of his practical interests comes to his hand, he spends long periods of time with it, going through it and thinking about what he reads.

The opportunity of the people of the village to hear the talk and observe the example of townspeople is much greater now than it was in 1931, but I cannot assert much as to the importance of this influence upon their lives. I should say that at least three times as many people from outside the village come to Chan Kom daily as did in 1931, when thirty-five persons were counted as coming to or through the village in ten days. Of course, many who come are from little settlements, rural villagers, like the people of Chan Kom. The traders and hog-drovers, in many cases persons who live in towns, are now commonplace in Chan Kom, and many more urban officials come to the village. The townsman brings a new manner of talk and behavior to the village; his easy language, his air of experience and authority, and his stories and comments about politics or distant adventure bring him an audience in Chan Kom. Lodging for a night or more with some leading citizen of the village, such a townsman may talk of his travels in Mexico or abroad or may sing songs to a pleased circle of listeners. The songs and the stories are both forms of expression out-

side the tradition of Chan Kom. The Indians tell stories of
quite another sort—folk tales and legends of wonderwork-
ing, of witchcraft, of the gods, of the ancient mythical
people—and they sing no songs. They admire the townsman's telling of salty and knowing anecdotes and the
flourish and posture of his singing, but they do not imitate
him.

The greatest importation of city people and city ways
into Chan Kom occurred in 1944–45 through the residence
in the village for about a year and a half of the ten people
constituting the cultural mission. Residing in the midst of
the villagers, this group was assigned the task of raising the
standard of life and providing cultural stimulation. Its
sphere of activity was a group of settlements around and
including Chan Kom. While the mission was there—I visited Chan Kom for one day in 1944—the village was a
lively place. The mere presence of so many loud and active
people, with the manners of the town, changed for a time
the general tone of the community. Instruction was going
on in carpentering, leatherworking, techniques of hygiene,
sewing, and other arts; walls of houses were adorned with
painted designs; domestic structures were overhauled or
improved; "cultural evening programs" were frequently
held, with recitations, dramatic skits, music, and song.

Nevertheless, the residue of accomplished change in the
ways of Chan Kom from this cultural flood is not impressive as one returns to the village in 1948. The two leatherworkers, already mentioned, continue the practical art
they learned from the mission, as do, although more rarely,
the youth who learned carpentry and the girls who learned
how to give hypodermic injections. The people's knowledge of musical instruments was considerably extended,
and several men, as reported in foregoing pages, learned
how to dig wells. But not one of the little raised stoves of
lime cement which the mission taught the people to build

is now in use, nor have any of the privies built been kept in repair. In the less practical, more purely expressive arts, the enduring accomplishments of the mission are almost nil. A few of the young women were put to work under direction of the mission artist in painting designs on the walls of masonry houses; no villager has done such a thing since the mission left. Some of the young people lament the cessation of "cultural programs" and dramatic productions; they express the wish that the schoolteacher would arrange more; but no one tries to provide a play or arrange a program of recitations. The boy who learned how to make and use simple puppets occasionally takes out and admires the little figures he shaped under guidance of the mission instructors, but he does not do anything else with them. The people who spoke of the cultural missionaries agreed that the village was very lively and gay when they were there. On the other hand, they wasted time, and some of them brought "bad habits" into the village, in bottle form. "They were partly good and partly bad." One man said, "My well, and some designs painted on my wall—that was what I got out of the mission." Of any indication that the mission had an interest in learning what the policy and goals of the village were and might be made to be, there is nothing in the reports brought to me.

What I know about the influence of the city upon the people of Chan Kom as a result of visits paid to it by villagers is derived only from the remarks made by those who have been there. Most of the men of the village have made one or more visits to Merida; included are many men who speak no Spanish. On the other hand, several of the leading citizens have never been there. Two men only have gone as far as Campeche, and no one from the village has been outside the peninsula of Yucatan. A few young men have been taken from neighboring settlements into the interior of Mexico by conscription into the national army, but as yet no one has gone from Chan Kom itself. In recent years two or three of the Chan Kom families have made trips to Progreso, simply to experience the delights of a port city and to see the ocean. Those returned to Chan Kom from excursions to Merida or Progreso are indefinite as to the pleasures or advantages derived from their trips; they speak of the many people, the electric lights, the water of the sea, the many objects in the shop windows. The carnival of Merida is known as the great event of urban entertainment, and some young people express the wish to attend; few have. No one has spoken of the movies with any particular interest. Perhaps a third of the men have been to the movies in the city, and some of the women; a portable moving-picture projector was once used by a teacher to show some films in Chan Kom. The attendance was poor. It was said to me, "We can see all those things without paying for them—horses, and people, and things going around."

Two or three young men, and two or three young women, have lived and worked for periods of months in one of the principal towns of the region or in Merida itself. But only one person born in Chan Kom had moved to the city to live at the time of our visit in 1948. This young woman married a young man from a town, who had learned something of the ways of the outside world through employment by archeologists at Chichen Itza and who took his wife from the village to the city where he had found employment. She is visited occasionally by her father; he finds the city unpleasantly confining. Another town-bred young man, having established himself maritally with another Chan Kom girl, this winter also made the move to Merida. The girl wept; so did her mother, partly at the separation, partly because of uncertainty as to life in the city. Her sister, who had lived several weeks in Merida herself, took a more cheerful view and spoke of the opportunities to visit, in Merida, or in Chan Kom. Most people are reluctant or even very fearful to consider a suggestion of a move to the city. The great expense of city life is often offered as a reason for this attitude. In short, it requires a town-bred husband to move a Chan Kom woman to the city; and even then the move will be on the whole deplored. On the other hand, there is one man of middle age who has long striven to give his children some of the education and some of the manners of the city. He has taken his family there on excursions, and now he has bought a lot on the outskirts of the city. His sons and daughters consider favorably the possibility that the family, or some of them, might some day move to the city. The father has been much influenced by Villa, and I think it is largely through this influence that he came to adopt a view toward his children that is strange in Chan Kom. This man and his wife, alone of the parents of the village whom I know, think of helping their children to understand and enjoy a better way of life than tradition affords; the mother made some effort to nurse her babies regularly, not whenever they cried, and gave them strained orange juice; those parents inquire anxiously as to the best way to care for their child so it may recover from a bad cold; they bring their children books—a very few—and want them to have what in other circles would be called "the advantages." The prevailing view in the village is that children should be useful to their parents, while the parents teach industry, sobriety, and obedience, and arrange for their marriage and if possible their economic security. It is this family alone of those of Chan Kom (with one other exception when a Protestant family for a short time tried to make the change but did not carry it through) that has adopted a Spanish surname in place of the Maya patronymic. All members of the immediate family call themselves by this Spanish surname, including the married son. On the other hand, when one of this family thinks of kinship with the many cousins, aunts, and uncles in the village, he or she says, "We are all ———" (giving the traditional and common Maya surname). The adoption of a Spanish surname is an expression of a tentative and incomplete identification with the ways of the city. It does not break down the solidarity of the extended family.

The world in which the thought and interest of the villagers occasionally moves, that world outside of the village and its satellite settlements, has, then, expanded slightly with travel to and from Chan Kom, with the knowledge brought by the school, the cultural mission, and the printed page. But, of all that is said or set forth by these instruments of a wider knowledge, most leaves no impress; most slips away again after it has been said or read, for there is not enough in the existing motivations of the people to serve to hold it permanently in their knowledge and concern. There is very little in the city that has any real and enduring meaning for these villagers.

If this is true for the city and the towns of Yucatan, it is of course far more true of the conceptions held by the people of the world outside Yucatan. Here there is haziness, acquaintance with names of places and people, occasional effort to understand some distant event of war or politics. We made no systematic attempt to explore this outer periphery of the villager's awareness. A report of spontaneous questions or remarks may serve to suggest its nature. In the following random assortment of such material, the mind of Don Eus is not represented. He understands more than does any other about the outside world, not because his opportunities to learn have been greater than those of many other men, but because of his real habit of reading and his inquiring mind.

An older man wants me to explain where is this Iraq and why was fighting going on there. Another asks if it is true that China is farther away than Turkey. How does one travel to get to "my pueblo"? Is Chicago one pueblo or a whole lot of them? What became of that leader of the Germans during the war—what was his name? Shown a picture of Gandhi and given his name, no one (except Don Eus) could identify him or recall the name or face. But Stalin's name is well known, and his reputation is unfavorable; when a local political officer was acting with rigor, a village critic asserted that the man was "acting like Stalin." A woman asks whether *hetz-mek* (the native ritual performed when first the child is carried on the hip) is made in my pueblo? Is there baptism? When we get home, will my wife be able to get someone to help her in the kitchen— are there *mestizas* there (women wearing folk costume and so suitable for domestic employment)?

Outside the circle of villages that depend upon Chan Kom and the similar circles that make up one or two adjacent *municipios*, the imagination of the people does not often go. When they do think about the towns or the one city of Yucatan, it is (with small exception mentioned above) without any purpose to move there. The impulse to emigrate, the spirit of pioneering, was spent in the settlement and the building of Chan Kom. The people are content in success; they are not restless. The many children are fed with the labor on the land and with the commerce that has now been added; there are no surplus sons that have to emigrate. The accumulated maize and other wealth makes Chan Kom secure as compared with other villages of the region. During the drought of 1942, people did not leave Chan Kom; they stayed to feed the hungry of neighboring settlements and to buy at low prices the gold chains and cedar washing boards of those who had no corn left.

Nor are the people seeking to attract the townsmen to settle in Chan Kom. They welcome as settlers hard-working Maya villagers. They are still of the opinion that the way of the *dzul* is not the way of the Indian and that the two kinds of people should live each in its own community. The teacher and his family are never fully within the village life; they are necessary anomalies; they bring troublesome problems, as when a marriage is suggested between a girl of such a family and a boy of the village. The old Mexican who now lives in Chan Kom is the exception that proves the rule. Outsider as he is, he works as the villagers do, attends the ceremonies, and labors on public works.

These villagers built their "road to the light" not that they should leave Chan Kom by it, nor yet that the city people should come to live among them. They built it so that their settlement might receive the benefits that would come to it from the towns. The road would make it easier for visitors and teachers and traders to come. It would bring townsmen who would show them how to grow useful fruit trees and to prevent or cure disease. It would bring musicians to Chan Kom so its life might be gayer, its festivals better attended. The road would make it possible for Chan Kom more easily to market its hogs, its poultry, and its surplus corn. It would be needed in the struggle for political dominance.

Plainly, the people of Chan Kom have realized the benefits they sought. They are practical benefits. They are additions to technology and wealth and also arts and knowledge that can be used in turn to increase skill, property, and power. Spanish is learned because it helps the people to continue along this road to practical achievement, and for this reason reading and writing are learned, and books are occasionally read.

With the new wealth and the new practical arts have come also along this road certain new customs and certain changes in manner: a taste for some of the products of the city and pleasure in excursions to the city; baseball; business; an enhanced respect for private property; increased confidence in meeting and dealing with city people; a degree of freedom of conduct in young people of both sexes.

What Chan Kom appreciates and enjoys is a little more varied than it was and is less exclusively fixed by the village tradition. The changes that have taken place in Chan Kom are not fully summed up by saying simply that its people have taken over tools and techniques of civilization. Tastes and manners, norms of the enjoyable and the good, have changed too.

In these respects the change is not great. But the general direction is significant. "The road to the light" starts out toward Chicago rather than toward Mexico City. The changes in Chan Kom are in the direction of North American or cosmopolitan urbanized life rather than in the direction of Latin culture. By learning Spanish, people in Chan Kom are enabled to read about scientific horticulture, child care, and the prices of commodities in foreign markets. The language has not so far been a way to Latin culture. The two zestful sports, business and baseball, are surely not Latin in nature or origin. And the added ease of manner of some of the young people is more congenial to the informality of North America than to the conventions of conservative Latin America.

Apparently the spirit of this people is not favorable to the adoption of Latin manners or mores. The villager listens to the romantic or dramatic songs of the visiting hog-drover, but he does not learn the words or the gestures. When a villager recites a traditional ritual utterance, he does so in a low gabble without gesture or facial expression. He has no inclination to expressive behavior or its cultivation as arts. The value which the Latin finds in the expression of the emotions is not shared by these Indians. Nor is the enjoyment or cultivation of sentiment. The "Day of the Mother," in which much sentiment is expressed about mothers and maternity, has found no lodging in the calendar of Chan Kom, nor do these people recite sentimental verse or admire sentimental postcards. The disinclination toward public revelation of feeling of any sort is manifest in the fact that (although simple gestures of respect of ancient Spanish origin are used in solemn ritual) the villagers have learned almost none of the Latin conventions of greeting: the conventional, often elaborate words of pleasure at meeting, let alone the *abrazo*—that double, half-embrace between good friends. Years ago teachers taught the people of Chan Kom to come out from behind half-closed doors at the entry to the village of a respected visitor and offer him a quick, limp handshake. But this is mostly gone now, and meetings and partings are unadorned with gesture or formal speech.

None of the aesthetic sensibility of Latin culture has found lodgment in the Chan Kom people. We never heard an aesthetic judgment expressed on anything in nature, and the praise given a work of practical art does not suggest any pronounced aesthetic component. The mural decorations, the dramatic performances, and the elocutionary art of the cultural mission were interesting to the villager but uncongenial to his own spirit; he has accepted the product, but he has not begun the cultivation of any fine art. (The dance music played, ponderous and emphatic, is of Spanish origin; like the crossing and gestured kissing of the rituals, it entered the village life long ago and was bent to the Indian gravity and distaste for individual flare.) Nor does the villager exhibit, or show any indication that he will exhibit, that revealed pride and sensitiveness to invasion of personal integrity which is characteristic of the Latin. His road goes in another direction. The practicality, the exaltation of hard work, and the acquisitive rather than the expressive spirit—these qualities of the villager lead him away from Latin culture toward another, perhaps a predominating stream of world-wide expanding influence. Before progress came to Chan Kom, Chan Kom had a life-view of its own, not at all Latin in nature, and Chan Kom has shaped the progress it has won in conformity with this ethos.

VIII

Chan Kom, Its Ethos and
Its Success

The influence of religion is not confined to the manners, but it extends to the intelligence of the people. . . . It reigns without obstacle, by universal consent; the consequence is . . . that every principle of the moral world is fixed and determinate, although the political world is abandoned to the debates and the experiments of men. Thus the human mind is never left to wander over a boundless field; and whatever may be its pretensions, it is checked from time to time by barriers that it cannot surmount. Before it can innovate, certain primary principles are laid down, and the boldest conceptions are subjected to certain forms which retard and stop their completion.[1]

THESE words were written not about Chan Kom but, by Alexis de Tocqueville, about another people who brought an established moral and religious order into a frontier: the people of the United States as they were in 1830. Like the Europeans who colonized the United States, the settlers of Chan Kom came into a little-occupied territory of open resources; like them, they were stimulated by ideas of liberty; like them, they brought with them a system of religious institutions and of moral ideas that continued to control their conduct in the new settlements. The connection had by the Chan Kom people with their country of origin—the villages to the north and east from which they came—is of course much closer than in the case of the North Americans, and the homogeneity of the population is greater. In both cases, however, "the imagination . . . is circumspect and undecided; its impulses are

1. Alexis de Tocqueville, *Democracy in America* (New York: Alfred A. Knopf, 1946), I, 304-5.

checked, and its work unfinished. These habits of restraint
recur in political society, and are singularly favorable both
to the tranquility of the people, and the durability of the
institutions it has established."[2] In Chan Kom everyone
knows what ought to be done about getting a wife, baptiz-
ing a child, maintaining a household, and performing the
novenas and agricultural and therapeutic ceremonies that
piety and prudence, through tradition, alike recommend.
The customs and the morality of the people's forefathers
are on the whole continued on the frontier; they still chan-
nel impulses, even while new inventions and arts from the
city are adopted, and ingenuity and enterprise are finding
new ways to wealth and to material advancement. The
only serious threat to the authority and uniform influence
of this moral tradition has been Protestantism, but even
this struck at the integrity of the community not so much
by throwing doubt on the rightness of the traditional ways
of life, though this was also involved, as by dividing the
families into two nonco-operative and even hostile groups.
The Protestant episode in Chan Kom was not so much a
war of dogma, a coming of heterodoxy, as it was an unsuccessful mutiny.

Indeed, the content of the traditional morality of these
pagan-Catholic Indians bears notable resemblance to that
of the Protestant American pioneers, as Tocqueville represents them. The respect for the tie of marriage, the order-
liness of family life, and especially the emphasis on industry are present in Chan Kom as on the North American
frontier. Of course there are important differences: the
longer-persisting authority of the father over the son, the
much greater dependence of young women, and the emphasis on discipline and obedience to authority, among many
other characteristics, make Chan Kom a different kind of
society from the United States in 1830. Yet in the general

2. *Ibid.*, p. 305.

reliance upon a stable and orderly family life and in the strong emphasis placed on productive industry as a virtue, with the acceptance of the principle that the task of manhood is to wrest a living from nature while maintaining a pious and prudential relation to God, there is much in the comparison.

In regarding industry, frugality, and productive effort as ends in themselves, in condemning idleness, in coming to view the increase of capital as a good for its own sake, these villagers had much of the Protestant ethic before ever they heard of Protestantism. Whether the strong emphasis on industry arose in the discipline of the Catholic mission of colonial times or in the forced labor of the hacienda, or whether its origins go back into the life of the natives before Columbus, I do not know; but certain it is that this virtue stands in the center of their scheme of values. It is what makes the Indian feel that in this at least he is superior to the *dzul*. The Indian can work, work, work, eat only a little atole and some dried tortillas, and endure the heat, the thorns, and the insects of the bush; but "the blood of the *dzul* is weak." In Chan Kom the church bells are rung an hour or more before dawn, and to the question, "Why?" the answer is given, "So as to wake everyone up." To rise early and go to the milpa or to the work of the household, this is the first injunction. To work, and not to waste, is the commandment. Under the influence of this virtue, progress was accepted in Chan Kom—a progress that cut down unproductive shade trees so that fruit trees might be planted, that sought "cultural programs" that would teach how to make poultry produce and how to make beekeeping profitable; that accepted the multiplication of cattle, money, and business as further expressions of the good life. The ethos of Chan Kom is practical and prudent. It stresses sobriety and obedience; it takes honesty for granted.

But it is a practical ethic that requires no promise or hope of salvation to support it. The people are not concerned with salvation. The villager is closer to Benjamin Franklin than he is to Wesley. He is concerned with earthly affairs; he sees the gods as rewarding men for their prudence and piety with good fortune on this earth and in this life. Piety and practical good sense are closely entwined; good husbandry is virtue, virtue hardly distinguishable from the virtues of domestic life and religious piety. To make the land produce and the cattle multiply is to be respected by men and to be blessed by God and the gods. "What is good is to care for the land as if giving affection to a wife and family," wrote Don Eus in a memorandum in which he strove to express his ideas as to the duty of man. The land is under the direct protection of the ever present supernaturals, watched by the *yuntzils*, blessed by God-Christ; so religion supports the leading virtues of industry, frugality, and endurance. The rewards, however, are here on earth.

With no history of money as an evil in the past of these people, with no teaching of the church of which they are aware as to the *turpitudo* of usury or profit, money and commerce came to Chan Kom easily, as a part of the opportunities and interests of the modern and progressive life. The qualities needed for economic success were already virtues in Chan Kom. In this its people were ready-made Calvinists. Don Eus wrote in many places in the margins of a book he reads, "*importancia de dinero*." The words are written opposite passages about industry, obedience, or the evils of fighting or of drunkenness. What is the importance which he sees in money? Is it not that he finds money a new measure of success as also of reward of virtue? Money is important to the men of Chan Kom, first, of course, as a way to store away one's future security (although here it is still second to corn); and then as a counter, a token, in a sort of moral game—the new activity of business and profit. Money is a good as associated with progress and as an evidence of the fruits of labor. The Chan Kom people spend little in consumption goods, and little of that in "conspicuous consumption." They accumulate their cattle, store away their maize against the bad years— and leave coins and bills in old tin cans or in little bundles on a shelf. In the frontier the old frugality and industry are developing into a phase of expansive enterprise, of incipient capitalism. Before the migration to Chan Kom the fathers of the present pioneers lived where resources were so limited as to make an ideal of economic expansion impossible. When the settlers moved out of this area of closed resources and enforced work for masters, they found new homes in a territory that offered not merely security but fresh opportunity. There they were stimulated to enterprise and further industry, for, serfdom over, the rewards went to the worker himself. The frontier contributed to the spirit of liberty and independence. It allowed the resourceful and the imaginative to come to the top; the excellent leaders that Chan Kom has had might not have been leaders had they stayed at home. It helped develop that passion for material advancement, for technical progress and material improvement, that has come to characterize the village.

The traditional morality was not Puritanism. It did provide an ethical and a religious basis for industry and for business endeavor. It frowned upon sexual indulgence, but it did not get excited about it; it did not make concupiscence a major sin. More generally, the Chan Kom morality, while sober and prudent in its tone, makes much more place for the life of pleasure than did Puritanism. With regard to dancing and enjoying the traditional fun and festivals, the *evangélicos* who came to convert Chan Kom were too Puritan for the ethos of Chan Kom. The ethos of Chan Kom is restrained rather than ascetic. To deny the flesh is not seen as a good in itself or as a means to grace—except as passions are incompatible with the sacredness which must attend ritual occasion and as therefore continence is enjoined at certain ceremonies—no, rather it is that drunkenness is wasteful, and sexual indulgence brings one a bad name. But to be happy, to enjoy a festival, music, or talk, are good things too. Baseball is a doubtful case; it is outside the traditions, and it wastes time and clothing.

The school, on the other hand, is too free with the traditional standards of personal and sexual morality for the ethos of Chan Kom. In this sector of the moral life it is Chan Kom that appears puritan and prudish to the city-trained teacher. The ethos of Chan Kom looks with suspicion on any innovation that invades the domestic life, that weakens the authority of fathers over sons, the subordination of wives to husbands and the identification of their interests with their husbands' interests, or that breaks in upon the sexual taboos and the ideas of decorum and decency. So the people feel disgust or fear at the suggestion that their children be seated together, girl and boy, in the school, and the romping of boys and girls suggests danger of sexual evil. Frankness in sexual matters will not come easily to Chan Kom.

Nothing in the ideas and examples offered by the city, except it be this freedom offered girls and boys in school, has seriously challenged the moderation and restraint of the traditional character of the people. Religion remains as it was: a fulfilment of ritual duties and the inconspicuous conduct of a life of labor and personal decency. There is little passion and no turmoil of the inner life in such a dutiful way. Religion is without intensive personal expression, without mysticism, and without revelation. An occasional visitor that comes to the village offers practical magic: one comes with a healing magnetic battery; another, traveling the countryside when first I saw this village, offered mysterious healing too, with herbs and laying-on of hands and the authority suggested by dark glasses and hair worn long. But there is no revivalism in religion; no "hawkers of God," such as came upon the American frontiersman to stir his spirit to vision and conversion, appear in these Maya villages. Protestantism, in so far as it reached these natives so as really to change their personal lives, reached those few who had been unable without the new teaching to realize traditional virtues: the wasteful, violent, and self-indulgent became, with the aid of the Protestant missionaries, as sober, or more sober, than their own ancient ethos told them to be.

So, while freedom is a conscious ideal of these people and a goal toward which they have striven during all these years, it is not a freedom of the spirit, not a liberation from taboo and ancient moral imperative, which they have sought, but freedom economic and political. Like the American pioneer, it was political life that remained open to exploit, adventure, and achievement. "The political world is abandoned to the debates and experiments of men." The Chan Kom people have for many years now debated their measures to make themselves a free and independent municipality, a village paramount over all its neighbors, and have worked and talked to this end, all in the name of progress and liberty. The background of their strong desires for liberty lies in the long centuries of serfdom. The older men know the stories of the hardships of this semislavery from their own fathers; there are some in Chan Kom who were themselves peons bound to their labor. Moreover, the story of the "War of the Castes," that bitter struggle between Indians and whites that lasted through the second half of the nineteenth century, is known in its essential outlines by the older people, at least, of Chan Kom. This was a war in which the Indians

strove to drive from the peninsula the race that had oppressed them. The Chan Kom people identify themselves
with the rebels; they quote the old phrases of contempt—
pek-dzul, "white man's dog"; or *ledz-plato*, "plate-licker"—
for those Indians who sided with the whites in the conflict.
The story of the great rebellion was told me one evening in
a group of men, with evident understanding that it was a
rebellion of the oppressed, that it grew from the harsh
treatment experienced by Indians on some haciendas. And
though they know the war ended inconclusively, with some
bands of Indians withdrawing to isolation in the forests of
the south and the others making their peace with the
whites, their past, they feel, was one of glorious revolution.

This revolutionary tradition, half-legendary in the
stories still told of the "War of the Castes," is continued in
the memories of the present-day people of Chan Kom concerning the revolution of 1917–21. Here was a fight for
freedom in which they themselves struck ringing blows.
The participation of the Cemes, the Pats, and the Tamays
in the battles of those years has been described by Don Eus
in that autobiography which he contributed to the book
about Chan Kom published in 1934. The little war they
fought was a war of freedom: the "Liberals" represented
the landowner and the vested interest; the Socialist party
stood for the worker, the Indian, the dispossessed. Felipe
Carrillo Puerto, José Maria Iturralde Traconis, and other
urban leaders aroused the Indians to warfare and then to
political action to achieve their freedom from serfdom and
the political independence of their village communities.
There filtered down to the Indians of the villages elements
of the great liberating movements of the Western world, a
diluted spirit of French and Russian revolution. The Indians shouted: "Long live liberty of the downtrodden
workers and death to the liberal assassins who do not wish
to work!" They addressed each other as "comrades," and

they wore red cockades in their hats. And when the civil war was won, and legal serfdom at least was ended and the principle of government for the people accepted, however imperfectly it came to be realized in the political institutions and practices of the years that followed, the people of Chan Kom turned to politics as the means to carry forward their successful revolution. They turned to the task of making their settlement into a pueblo: a community with the form and the practical advantages of civilized life, with its own lands to exploit for the benefit of those who worked them, and with the freedom and the right to make its own government and administer its laws through its own citizens. The grant of *ejidos* was the first of the postwar political victories. Next, the "free municipality" became the goal of their collective effort, and this goal was reached, it may be remembered, in 1935. Chan Kom had its success. This success has always been defined, be it noted, in terms of the local community, the village, only. The political aspirations of Chan Kom do not go beyond the village and the settlements near by that have been drawn into its orbit and have become part of its *municipio*. Nationalism is too large a loyalty for the people of Chan Kom. Even the state government is thought of, as is the national government, as an outside authority, a source of help as a seat of punishing power. For neither of these larger political entities does the villager feel that he is responsible. Where the frontiersman to whom Tocqueville talked was an American, the Chan Kom native, illiterate and far more isolated, with a long tradition of largely independent village communities, is a citizen of Chan Kom. It is liberty for himself and for his village for which he has struggled. The fraternity he feels is for his fellow-villager and, to less degree, for other Maya villagers of that part of Yucatan.

In the sharing of rights and duties among all members of the village community, Chan Kom is a democracy. It is a democracy in the sense that it is not an aristocracy, in the sense that equality of opportunity on the whole prevails and is valued, and in that the affairs of the community are regarded as the responsibility of all its members. In Chan Kom there are no classes of hereditary privilege; while men strive to provide for the material security of their children, no rights or advantages are accorded by law or custom by virtue of birth in one kind of family rather than another. Even the richest in Chan Kom have known poverty, and their relative wealth is the result of their own industry and enterprise. The rich and the poor live similar lives, with similar tastes; the poor strive to get rich, and, when they do, they add those comforts of life which were added by those who became rich before them. Labor for public services (*fagina*) is required of all, and, when important matters of common concern require decision, a general assembly is held. "It is not only a portion of the people which is busied with the amelioration of its social condition, but the whole community is engaged in the task; and it is not the exigencies and the convenience of a single class for which provision is to be made, but the exigencies and the convenience of all ranks of life."[3]

Nevertheless, Tocqueville would not find proclaimed in these bush settlements the other of those twin principles that he found so loudly and confidently proclaimed in the early United States—democracy. Freedom, economic and political freedom, is an ideal and a goal, but little is said in Chan Kom about equality, fraternity, or democracy. It is the Golden Rule, applied very locally, rather than any general principle that all men are born equal, that guides Chan Kom. "The peace and tranquillity of all beings on earth," wrote Don Eus, "depends solely on respecting the rights and reasonable nature of one's neighbor as one's self; this is the old law of our Lord God. So my deceased father, Don

3. *Ibid.*, p. 249.

Diego Ceme, and my deceased father-in-law, Don Asuncion Pat, used to say." And he added in the next words: "For me the proof of this lies in the fact that here is Chan Kom, in the heart of the bush. Before there were only four or five thatched houses; now in appearance it compares, in its category of Independent Municipality, with the pueblos of the ancients."

While men are to have equal opportunities, they are not to participate equally in political life. Chan Kom conceives of a hierarchy of power and responsibility, in which each man does the duty assigned him. Government, to them, is not a meeting of men who look each other levelly in the eye and in which each voice and vote counts as every other. Government is a fatherly discharge of responsibility by the powerful and the able for the benefit of all but with lesser men taking lesser places. This is the view which tradition gives the native of the heavenly world: it is a hierarchy, of saints and angels, with God at its apex, and in this hierarchy fit too, albeit somewhat vaguely, the *yuntzils*, the beings of rain cloud, cenote, and forest. Every major authority has his assistant, his *noox*, and under every major authority are subordinated authorities, and so on down. Obedience, without discussion of whys and wherefores, is a duty. Those who have the duty and the right of assuming the principal offices are those who have reached years of discretion and have proved that discretion by sobriety, good judgment, and industry.

It may be added that they have now proved their worth also by wealth, the recent fruit of industry. The viewpoint of the native with regard to political democracy is made plain in the way in which a local government is formed. It consists of five major officers, who are elected, and twenty-four officers of constabulary. (The number of these is fixed by law proportionate to the number of family heads; they are ranked in four ranks with military names.) These of ficers of constabulary are chosen by the chief of the five principal officers, the municipal president. They are dependent upon him and are required to obey him. When a new government is to be formed, according to state or national law, the municipal president calls a meeting of the five principal officers and the eighteen officers of constabulary (all, excepting the six of lowest rank who are boys). These twenty-three men prepare a slate of officers to nominate as candidates for election. Once the slate is formed, there are no rival candidates; the names chosen appear on ballots furnished by the outside government, as nominees of the political party associated with the state government. At a later meeting, the *comisarios*, officers of government in the dependent pueblos of the *municipio*, are given the slate to approve; this is their share in the proceedings.

The proposal of a slate at the first meeting is made by one of the recognized leaders of the community, perhaps by the municipal president himself. Informal discussions have taken place among the principal leaders, and it is clear, in most cases, who will be nominated when the meeting occurs or within what very limited choice the nominations will be made. Electioneering may go on in advance of this meeting by an ambitious man, who, desiring to be municipal president, may offer drink and promises to the *comandantes*, *sargentos*, and *caporales* who will vote at the nominating convention. The leaders, however, are careful to put up for nomination men who have property. Such men, it is felt, will stand for law and order; they will have influence as well as will to prevent or to stop disputes; they will be respected. So the making of a slate is largely determined by the judgments of a few elder men, established leaders; the eighteen men of the constabulary will contribute their votes but are not likely to go against the judgment of a few united leaders. At a recent meeting to nominate candidates, two candidates were proposed for municipal president. The man supported by the three or four major leaders of the community was nominated by a vote of seventeen to three (three men were absent). Voting is by voice. This nomination is, of course, tantamount to election; the casting of ballots, by such citizens as care to do so, is formal.

This method of making a government is supported by the village leaders. One said: "I do not know that it is good to give the responsibility of running the village to all the people. I doubt that it is. There aren't enough people who are really able to manage public affairs. Chan Kom grew in the middle of the woods." Certain other villages of the territory, under influence from the city, have adopted a method of nominating candidates for local offices in a general assembly by nomination "from the floor" by any citizen. Leaders of Chan Kom have watched such proceedings, which have in cases resulted in acrimonious discussion and even violence, and they are sure that their way is better.

The success of Chan Kom is thus in part harmonization of the new economic and political opportunities with the traditional moral conceptions and the traditional scheme of society. The accumulation of wealth and the making of money expressed the central need for security from want and the ancient virtue of industry. The old pattern of competition among local communities, in war, religion, and land dispute, found new outlets in business rivalry and political struggle. The teacher and the cultural missionary brought the literacy and the practical arts that were needed in acquiring the new wealth and achieving success in the new forms of competition. And when the examples offered by the city world were too far from the tradition and conceptions, the people of Chan Kom, often after going forward, drew back, to consolidate their position with the old virtues. The girls might go to school to learn to write and to sew, and perhaps to wear, the new clothing; but they might not learn to speak freely with boys. The reading of the Bible taught by the Protestants—with later doubts— was approved as opening a path to wisdom and sound guidance. But it was not found wise to give up the old festivals and the old grave pleasures; and it was found very unwise for Chan Kom to become an isolated sect among neighboring settlements adhering to the old way. The revolutionary leadership was accepted, for the freedom from domination and from poverty it brought, but it was not followed to the point of open voting by all in a public assembly. This was a conception too bold for Chan Kom. It was "subjected to certain forms which retarded and stopped" its completion. In political and administrative organization Chan Kom remains a community led by the enlightened, the responsible, and the practically successful; it is still a paternalism; its solidarity is hierarchical; it rests on virtues and a social structure that are ancient and enduring.

The successful management of the transformations that have occurred in the community have demanded able leadership. There have been many crises to pass through. One was the unwillingness of the unprogressive citizens to make the sacrifices required in early days to convert Chan Kom into a pueblo and the necessity to discipline these reluctant ones or to force them to leave the village. A second crisis arose out of the competition and hostility of other villages that strove to prevent the political success of Chan Kom. A third crisis, which almost overturned the local leadership of Chan Kom, developed from the devisive influence of the Protestant movement. And a fourth kind of situation which was involved in the Protestant episode and which is perennially and increasingly critical is the tendency of the family groups to become hostile to one another. Upon this rock has many a village ship of state split in these southeastern forests. All these situations, and especially the factional problems, have called for wise leaders.

Of them firmness has been required at one time, compromise and conciliation at another. The leaders have made mistakes, but they have been quick to pull back when they have gone too far in one direction, adroit in making use of representatives of the principal families, and determined— very, very determined—upon their course. If Don Eus Ceme had not been one of these leaders, one would be writing about others, for there are other good leaders in Chan Kom. He is, however, an extraordinarily able man, and so stands out. Sylvanus G. Morley has already recorded this about him.[4]

The explanation of the success of Chan Kom, among other settlements in its neighborhood that started even with it, does not seem to lie in any advantages of location or of natural resources. Chan Kom was situated on no important path or crossroads; it became an important crossroad in the bush after it became an important village. The land about Chan Kom is poor and thin; the engineer who first surveyed it so described it. No explanation for its success appears in anything except the accident of the competence of its first settlers and, thereafter, in the proverbial successfulness of success. A military governor in Valladolid received reports as to the sobriety and honesty of the people of Chan Kom; so he sent the village a schoolteacher. Later, urban leaders of Mexico's "revindicating revolution" stimulated the settlers to make the effort to rebuild the village and to earn a grant of communal lands. Chance, again, put into the village a teacher who was interested and sympathetic enough to remain for several years, helping the people to attain their now-forming political and social objectives. The enterprise of the village and the presence of this teacher drew to it the American archeologists, the writer of these lines, and a good many other American or Mexican city people. Something about Chan Kom ap-

4. *The Ancient Maya* (Stanford, Calif., 1946), pp. 28–29.

peared in Merida newspapers. When the federal government came to choose villages as centers of influence for the cultural missions they were sending out, Chan Kom, now known so favorably for what its inhabitants had already accomplished, became one of these centers. But although outside influences have played upon this settlement more than upon any other settlement of the region, the fact remains that as these outsiders brought as much trouble as they brought help, as many problems to solve as they brought knowledge with which to solve them, it was the skill and perseverance of the villagers themselves that achieved success. The villagers recognize these changes as success. The principal men sit in the evening in the plaza and speak with satisfaction of the great number of cattle that come, bellowing, to be watered. They reminisce about past political struggles, and they give judicious advice to men who come to them from lesser settlements with similar troubles of their own. They admire their masonry houses, the new church, and the new school, and perhaps they express regret that the two open-air theaters are so little used. When the bands are playing, and the sound of Chan Kom's heavy gaiety reaches far out into the bush, they are greatly satisfied. As they talk, some man may bring up the question, recently discussed, as to bringing a radio to the village, with a loud speaker in the middle of the plaza.

The people know, too, that there is less sickness and that more of their children live to maturity. They have a comfortable feeling from the accumulation of corn in their private granaries: Chan Kom can withstand two successive years of drought. Nor is there any problem of crime; no one could tell me of any crime in Chan Kom itself in recent years. We had in 1948 no experience of even the most trifling theft by children. In lesser settlements, of backward people, there may be killing of stolen cattle for food and occasional personal violence under the influence of liquor. In Chan Kom, however, "property is respected," and— with unfortunate exceptions which are generally regretted and then more or less hushed up—people do not get violently drunk.

Substantially lacking, too, is that index of the anxieties of Yucatecan communities: witchcraft. The belief that there is witchcraft appears undiminished in Chan Kom as compared with 1931; but there is no more of it now than then. We were able to learn of only a single case of asserted witchcraft; when the Chan Kom girl who broke her incompleted engagement to a boy of another village so as to marry a boy of Chan Kom fell sick, the *h-men* who attended her told her parents that the jilted youth was sending witchcraft into her. But witchcraft directed by one of Chan Kom against another of Chan Kom is no more likely now than it was in those earlier years.

But not in Chan Kom, any more perhaps than anywhere else, is success complete, is victory final. The few people who think about the condition of their community, those who look beyond their private problems to those of the entire village, are anxious about the future. They see not only success but also difficulty. The very achievement of the success they sought has brought about new dangers which, in the early days of their planning, they did not foresee. They see them now and think how best to deal with them.

There is the obvious impoverishment of the land. They know that the yield of corn from the fields they plant has gone down during the years covered by this report by one-third to one-half. And corn is still the staff of life and the principal money crop. The people see the reason—or part of the reason—for this decline writ upon the changing face of the country they inhabit: where once large trees grew tall and thick, now the bush is small and sparse. The trees are cleared too often. "Now there is no more high bush."

Nor are there now any considerable pockets of rich moist soil where sugar and pineapples can be grown. During the winter of these observations a man came from a settlement lying to the south where there is still high bush and where the soil holds more water to buy from a man of Chan Kom his sugar press and copper sugar kettle; they had long been lying in Chan Kom unused. Moreover, people plant fewer orange, lime, and banana trees than they used to; it is harder to get fruit in the village today than it was seventeen years ago. The answer as to why so few fruit trees are planted is sometimes given that "it is too much trouble." It is, I think, because cattle and commerce bring faster and greater returns—and their development is a more interesting activity.

One man said, "We are living by trade, and from much cattle. What we have much of now in Chan Kom is children. In every house there are many children. Many children, little work, and little intelligence." The people see the population press upon the resources. So far as they speculate as to remedies, they turn to the possibility of increasing resources. Don Eus sees a hope in diversified agriculture. He reads about this in little educational news sheets sent out by the state authorities concerned with agrarian matters. So out in a new clearing made in the bush he plants fruit trees, beans, and several kinds of the starchy root crops long known in Chan Kom. He has moved his poultry to this rural settlement; there he corrals his cattle and keeps his horses. The land there is better than it is directly around Chan Kom. He thinks that there he may provide for his several married sons and his many grandchildren. If he cannot do it alone, the authorities in the city will give him help again, as they have helped the people of Chan Kom in earlier years. He wrote, in a memorandum to me: "Yet if we work the land well and plant fruit trees, the land will provide everything. But now everything is done wrong; the people make only milpas. We must modernize our agriculture. If we do not, great ruin and misery will follow." And then with a turn of thought that expresses again the persisting intermingling, throughout the history of the village, of self-reliance and dependence on outside help: "It depends on the government to save the fields."

There are several other men in Chan Kom who share the fears of Don Eus and something of his view as to the measures which should be taken. A notable development of the last dozen years is the establishment, in rural places from two to five miles from Chan Kom, of little private agricultural establishments that are also residences, or half-residences, of the men who have built them. In an earlier chapter it was explained how the law that assures individual rights over plots developed within the *ejidos* makes these new establishments possible. So far there are only three or four men who have made them, and that of Don Eus is the best developed. But several other of the older men spend increasing amounts of time out in these bush settlements. They say that they are caring for their cattle. They are also planting root crops and fruit trees. And they are getting away from Chan Kom. The younger people, married and independent, seem to accept the increasing liveliness and crowdedness of Chan Kom; no one of them has moved back into the bush. One young married man—the skeptic as to *loh* ceremonies and treatments by the *h-men*—has, however, dug a well and fenced a tract of land just outside the village, where the road from the west enters. He says that later he will move his poultry and his hogs out there. He says that it is not good for them any more in the village—they do not have enough room. He hopes his son, when he grows up, may want to move to this suburban spot.

In the cases of the older men who are building establishments in the bush, there is clearly represented the impulse to get away from Chan Kom. Satisfied though they are

with the cattle and the people, with the glaring heat of the
stone houses, the tree-stripped plaza with its baseball diamond and its two unused theaters, with the clamor of the
motors that run the mills and the loud glory of Chan
Kom's own brass bands, they are glad from time to time to
get away from it all. The old reciter of prayers is now most
of the time out in the bush. Another old leader spends more
and more time at a rural settlement of his making. These
men cannot, or do not, articulate the motives that send
them there; perhaps they cannot express them even to
themselves.

Don Eus is quite clear about it. He knows that he is
making a retreat out at Ticincacab, where the land is high
and the breeze can blow over a man and over the rising
grove of rustling banana plants. He knows from what he is
retreating. There he brings his family to work and to pass
the night. He, who more than anyone made Chan Kom
great and progressive, sees a dark future for his village.
Things will be bad for the children of Chan Kom when
they grow up, he says, for two reasons: the land does not
produce as it did and the people are taking up vices and
bad habits. People are drinking more than they did, he
thinks. He says that when the present leaders of Chan
Kom are dead, without their good example the people will
become drunkards, as they are in some other villages.
Cigarette-smoking and chewing gum—even the recent fad
of wearing dark glasses—he sees as "vices," as wasteful and
corrupting customs unsuitable to a sound people. "And
then there is the great vice of idleness. People do not develop their own property; they are content to live by working for others. No one makes *sosquil* [twine of henequen
fiber] any more, or makes ropes. The ropes we use now are
bought in Merida."

Don Eus begins to look with disfavor on the wealth and
comfort which he has worked so hard to bring to his village.

In a memorandum to me he records his opinion that the masonry houses are bad for people. Inside them they keep away from the health-giving sun and the beneficial exposure to the elements. He compares those who stay in masonry houses to the pallid plants that grow in dark places. And he writes that the good foods that people are getting nowadays are bad for them too. "It is like a hog that by just eating, drinking, and lying in the shade or scratching himself is dying from his rich food and his lying around." And he expresses this view in spite of the traditional viewpoint that associates some corpulence with the beautiful and the desirable.

Don Eus it was who induced his fellow-villagers to build a straight wide road to Chichen and the outside world. Today the question is when and at what point the road from Chan Kom is to be joined with the highway along which pass trucks and busses from the city. About this Don Eus says: "When the road comes here, as it will, there will be more 'vices' here. There will be a movie in Chan Kom. Then every week the children will want to go, and if one goes, all the family must go. If one has six or eight children, it will be a great expense. The movie will become something that they will have to have, like food. It will happen with the movie as it happened with baseball: it is something they will have to have.

"There will be commercial singers of songs (*cancioneros*) in Chan Kom—another bad thing. All the children will listen to the songs sung, and come to get money from their fathers to buy the songs. The *cancionero* will sing a song, and sell the leaflet for twenty centavos. Then there will be another song, and another twenty centavos.

"Wherever roads come, the villages grow poor. Where there are vices and commercial pleasures (*diversiones*), there is poverty. When the road comes to Chan Kom, there will be a tavern there.

"So I have made my place at Ticincacab. There we can live soundly, taking care of the gardens and the cattle."

In the year of these observations the village stands at a resting place in the effortful course of its progress. The goal set a generation ago is reached, and no new goal has been defined to organize the community for further effort. It is hard to see what new effort could unite the forces of the community in an effort as sustained and as effective as that which has been made. There is no political status open to a rural village higher than that of the independent municipality. Furthermore, in achieving this status, in becoming the dominating settlement of a circle of settlements, Chan Kom has made its political organization coincide with the world of its traditional attachments and personal loyalties. As far as the sense of common responsibility could reach, so far is Chan Kom now responsible. To go outside the *municipio* for attachment of ambitions and recognition of responsibilities, the people would have to think of themselves as leaders in the world managed by the *dzul*. They would have to become political leaders of the state of Yucatan. And this would require an extension of their sense of solidarity and a breadth of social and political purpose which they are far from having. What changes within the community would be concomitant with the attainment of such a wider sense of group-belonging is something on which to speculate. They would have to be great. Without such a basis in enlarged interest, there is no immediate further political purpose to hold the people together. As the reader has, I hope, come to understand, it has been this objective, this determination to make Chan Kom a pueblo, that has provided the energy for the collective effort and enabled the leaders to unite the people. Without this common cause, without the stimulus of competition of other villages in the struggle for power, it will be harder to compose the inevitable disputes of factions and families.

In this year the community is still held in the leadership

of the men who made the effort just ended, and no transfer
to younger leaders has yet been made. The older leaders
tire and turn away from the uncertain future; they turn
back to the good earth and the ancient gods. Their influence, however, still predominates; most of the men who
formed the determination to make Chan Kom a pueblo are
still alive. In every one of the principal families at least one
man of that founding generation is still alive, working, giving advice, issuing orders to his sons, unmarried and married. There is no evidence of rebellion on the part of the
younger generation. They continue, as these pages have
recorded, to work the milpa and perform the ceremony.
Whether they will continue to do so when their fathers are
dead is of course a question critical in judging the future of
Chan Kom. They do not all continue to perform all the
ceremonies, and they, much more than their fathers, are inclined to choose first the medicine of the city or the urban
example as to costume and conduct. Without the paternal
authority and influence, no doubt they will feel freer to
neglect the old and establish the new. And the commerce
they now carry on affords them leisure and an opportunity
to go to the city that they did not have before. Don Eus
feels sure that there will be great changes, for the worse,
when he and his age-mates are gone—"the people will become drunkards" is his way of expressing a more general
fear of decline in moral standards.

So far, if one looks below the surface of wealth and material possessions, the changes in Chan Kom have not
been great. As compared with the transformations of
American society in a corresponding period of the nineteenth century, they are probably less marked. A much
less restless people than the Americans, a people limited
both by a narrow horizon of knowledge and interest and
also by folk culture, the people of Chan Kom have,
chiefly, enlarged the little circle of their economic and political power. They have no sense of destiny to make a con-

tinent theirs. There has been no urban or industrial revolution to break apart their traditional moral order.

Nevertheless, the prediction of Don Eus is probably
right. The young people who will take over Chan Kom
show no disposition to revive, to cultivate, or to enforce the
older standards. Their slowly changing interests attach to
the business, the purchases, the pleasures, and the tastes
of the town. They will go forward, for forward is the only
way they have to go. And therefore they will have to deal
with the dissensions and confusions which will attend further change. The road will come to Chan Kom, and the
young people from Chan Kom will leave it for the city.
Then it will be hardly possible to maintain the old faith
and to carry on, in a spirit of piety, the old rituals. To us,
in a day much later than that in which Chan Kom now
stands, and yet a day that is somehow in the same general
calendar of civilization, it is perhaps surprising to read in
Tocqueville how that acute visitor to us in 1830 was struck,
first and foremost, by the authority of religion in the life of
America. Continuance of the authority of religion is no
more than it was to us assured to the people of Chan Kom.
They will have to deal with the problems of the coming
generations, although they will not be so fortified with the
sense of conviction as to the good life as were their parents.
On the other hand, they will get even more help than their
parents had from education and the practical arts. They
will have to meet the future with less of faith to help them
and more of science.

The people of Chan Kom are, then, a people who have no
choice but to go forward with technology, with a declin-
ing religious faith and moral conviction, into a dangerous
world. They are a people who must and will come to identify their interests with those of people far away, outside
the traditional circle of their loyalties and political responsibilities. As such, they should have the sympathy of
readers of these pages.

Glossary

ALUX—A mischievous, goblin-like supernatural being associated with the artifacts of the ancient Maya.

BALAM—A supernatural being guarding milpa, village, or forest.

CABEÇERA—The seat of principal local government of a *municipio*.

CARGA—Unit of weight for corn and other commodities.

CATRÍN, CATRINA—One dressing in the garb of the city, not wearing the folk costume.

CENOTE—Natural well formed by collapse of the limestone crust of the land.

COMISARIO—Principal (elected) political officer of a pueblo.

COMPADRE—One who acted as godfather of my child, or the father of a child whose godfather I am.

CUARTEL—Building used for affairs of government in a pueblo or town.

DE VESTIDO—Wearing the garb of the city, not the folk costume.

DZUL—One not a Maya villager, a "white" person of town or city.

EJIDO—Collectively owned lands of a village or town, recognized by the state.

EJIDATARIO—One sharing rights in collective lands of a village or town.

FAGINA.—Labor on public works traditionally required of citizens in a village.

HETZ-MEK—Ceremony to assure proper development of a child performed in first year when it is first carried on the hip.

H-MEN—Shaman priest; specialist in Maya ritual, religious or therapeutic.

HUIPIL—Woman's long loose blouse; a part of the folk costume.

JARANA—Folk dance of Yucatan (derived from the Spanish *jota*).

JÍCAMA—A starchy tuber, *Pachyrhizus erosus* (L.) Urban.

MAESTRO CANTOR—Specialist in reciting Catholic prayers and in leading Catholic ritual.

MAZEHUA—A word used by the Indians to distinguish themselves from non-Indians.

MECATE—Unit of measure of land, about one twenty-fifth of a hectare.

MESTIZO—In Yucatan, one wearing the folk costume.

MILPA—Cornfield; a clearing in the bush where maize is planted.

MILPERÍO—A group of huts built at milpas for temporary occupancy by those working them.

MILPERO—One working a milpa; rural agriculturalist.

MUHUL—Costume, jewelry, and other traditional gifts to a bride from the bridegroom's family; delivery of the *muhul* seals the agreement to marry.

MUNICIPIO—An area and an organization of local government, containing one or more settlements and the rural territory between.

NOVENARIO—A novena; nine consecutive nights of prayer.

NOVIA—Sweetheart.

RANCHERÍA—A small settlement of a political category inferior to that of a pueblo.

TERNO—The fine dress of a village woman, for marriage and festal attire.

YUNTZIL—A general term for the supernaturals of Indian tradition.

Index